ALL-TERRAIN PUSHCHAIR WALKS
South Lakeland

Norman Buckley

© Norman Buckley, 2004. *Reprinted 2005*
Reprinted 2006, 2007 with minor amendments. Reprinted 2008
Reprinted 2009 with minor amendments

All Rights Reserved. No part of this publication may be reproduced, stored in a retrieval system, or transmitted in any form or by any means – electronic, mechanical, photocopying, recording, or otherwise – without prior written permission from the publisher or a licence permitting restricted copying issued by the Copyright Licensing Agency, 90 Tottenham Court Road, London W1P 0LA. This book may not be lent, resold, hired out or otherwise disposed of by trade in any form of binding or cover other than that in which it is published, without the prior consent of the publisher.

Published by Sigma Leisure – an imprint of
Sigma Press, Stobart House, Pontyclerc, Penybanc Road, Ammanford, Carmarthenshire SA18 3HP

British Library Cataloguing in Publication Data
A CIP record for this book is available from the British Library

ISBN: 978-1-85058-817-7

Typesetting and Design by: Sigma Press, Ammanford, Carms

Cover photograph: Biskey Howe viewpoint, near Bowness *(Norman Buckley)*

Maps: Bute Cartographics. Reproduced from Ordnance Survey mapping on behalf of The Controller of Her Majesty's Stationery Office. © Crown Copyright. Licence Number MC 1000320588

Photographs: Norman Buckley

Printed by: Bell & Bain Ltd, Glasgow

Disclaimer: the information in this book is given in good faith and is believed to be correct at the time of publication. No responsibility is accepted by either the author or publisher for errors or omissions, or for any loss or injury howsoever caused. Only you can judge your own fitness, competence and experience. Do not rely solely on sketch maps for navigation; we strongly recommend the use of appropriate Ordnance Survey (or equivalent) maps.

Preface

Access for as many people as possible to as much of the countryside as possible, even including mountainous areas, is very much a present day objective. To this end, various bodies have been and remain active in creating 'wheelchair' paths and in removing many of the obstacles such as high and difficult stiles which had previously prevented access to those with disabilities and/or accompanied by young children. The author's 'Level Walks' series of walking guide books is also a move in the same direction, suggesting a wide variety of routes in hilly areas without serious ascent and generally at the easier end of the walking spectrum.

The advent of the 'All-Terrain Pushchair' has greatly extended the frontiers for those with babies and young children, with comparatively easy passage over rough tracks, both stony and muddy, and the safe negotiation of steep slopes, up and down.

It follows that a book such as this, selecting and recommending suitable routes for ATP walkers in the outstanding holiday and walking area of the southern part of the Lake District, is performing a useful service. This is true both for parents (and possibly grandparents!) in discovering or rediscovering the magnificent countryside and, of at least equal importance, in introducing children at a very young age to those same delights.

Norman Buckley

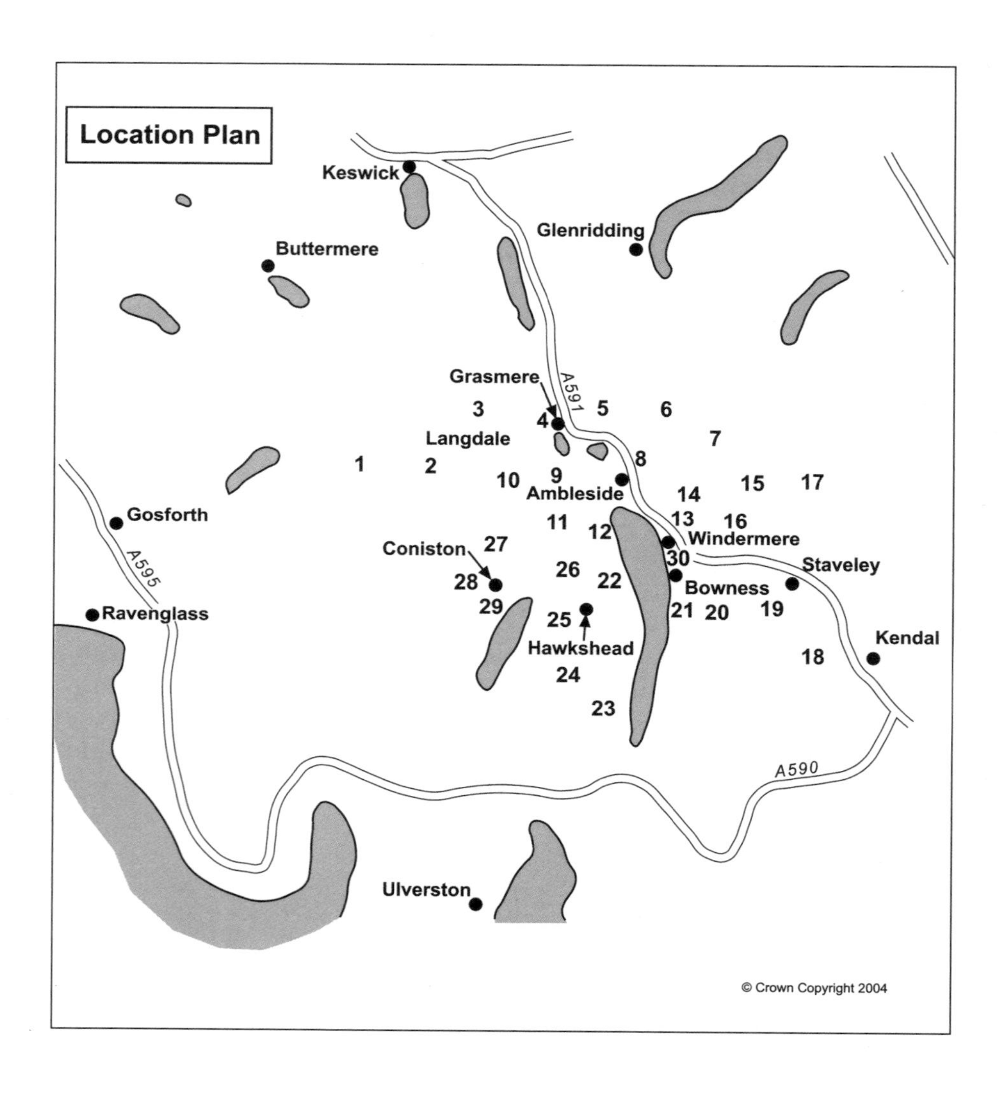
Location Plan
Keswick
Glenridding
Buttermere
Grasmere
A591
3
4
5
6
Langdale
7
8
1
2
10
9
Ambleside
15
17
14
Gosforth
11
12
13
16
Windermere
Coniston
27
30
Staveley
A595
26
22
28
Bowness
29
25
21
20
19
Ravenglass
Kendal
Hawkshead
18
24
23
A590
Ulverston
© Crown Copyright 2004

Contents

The Routes

Introduction

This book contains thirty recommended walking routes, many with variations, some circular and some out-and-back. They are set out on the location plan preceding the contents pages. In making this selection from the great number of walks available in the southern part of the Lake District, assumptions have been made. Firstly, that even strong and experienced country walkers will be looking for shorter walks when coping with a pushchair. The likely needs of the baby or young child will likewise militate against long excursions. Secondly, that habitual 'peak-baggers' will settle for less ambitious ascents in these circumstances.

So – the walks range from 2km (1¼ miles) to 9.5km (6 miles) in length, with a total ascent of no more than 200m (656ft). Within these parameters, the widest possible variety of Lakeland countryside has been included.

Routes and Grades

The format is that each walk has an introductory section, which includes distance, total ascent, start/car parking place, relevant Ordnance Survey map and refreshments (if any). There is also a brief description of the area, highlighting features of likely interest. Most important is an assessment of the route relative to the use of an ATP. At the risk of both over-simplification and subjectivity, a grading in the range of 1 to 5 is applied to the summation of the difficulties. **Grade 1** would be appropriate for a stroll of up to two or three miles on a broad level track along the Windermere shore. **Grade 5** would indicate either a longer walk with moderate difficulties or perhaps a walk with steep ascents, probably over rough stony surfaces. Factors involved are the state of the surface of paths and tracks, the extent and/or steepness of gradients and the presence or otherwise of other obstacles such as steps, tight gates and narrow bridges. Routes involving stiles and/or tight kissing gates are generally avoided. Even on the best footpaths and bridleways, some ponding water and mud is always likely to be found. With a pushchair it is more difficult to find an alternative route round wet patches; after periods of rain this could pose an unexpected problem.

Taken in conjunction with the accompanying narrative, this grading should enable a quick judgement to be made concerning the suitability or otherwise of a route. In some cases, advice is given that two adults are required to cope with an ATP. The route of the walk is then described fully, with an accompanying sketch plan.

Single and Double All-Terrain Pushchairs from the 'Mountain Buggy' range. *Reproduced by permission of Chariots All Terrain Pushchairs www.pushchairs.co.uk*

All-Terrain Pushchairs

Several makes of ATP are available, all with a wide range of accessories; first-time buyers should decide on their needs and then examine as many models as possible. Common features include a three-wheel format (although the front wheel may be double); large (at least 12") wheels with pneumatic tyres; quick-release system for the wheels; easy folding for carrying in a car boot; comprehensive weather protection, including waterproofing; and a good braking system. Some variables are the weight and size of the ATP, open or folded;

capacity for one or two children; lockable swivel or fixed front wheel(s); adapters for carrying very young babies; extra insulation for the feet; suspension. All should be supplied with a hand pump for tyre inflation and a basic puncture repair kit. Obviously a 'test-drive' with passenger is highly desirable, although a showroom floor hardly provides a realistic challenge!

Weather Protection

Parents will hardly need reminding that, even in warm weather, children in push chairs need much more warm cover than the adults who are working hard to push the ATP, possibly uphill. One-piece garments have obvious advantages in this regard. Don't forget hands and toes!

Adult Wear

Basically, the requirements are the same as for walking without an ATP. For these easy walks, trainers will suffice in most cases, although it must be said that large rocks, loose smaller stones, tree roots and clinging mud will all be encountered underfoot. For many, including the author, only hill-walking boots, with moulded soles, are acceptable in these circumstances.

In the Lake District, waterproof outer garments are always required, either worn or carried.

Precautions

Most of the walks in this book are short and, without a pushchair, would be very undemanding. They would hardly warrant the precautionary advice which is sensibly given to those who are undertaking mountain ascents and treks across remote areas. However, it makes sense to be a little over-cautious when accompanied by young children:

- ☆ Check the weather forecast; being caught in sudden heavy rain, snow or thunderstorms is, at best, thoroughly unpleasant and, at worst, could be dangerous.
- ☆ Carry a mobile phone (but don't rely on reception in the more mountainous areas).
- ☆ Carry a basic first-aid kit.

- ☆ Always have cold drink available.
- ☆ Carry some high energy food, both for the adult(s) and, of course, for the child(ren).
- ☆ Don't be too ambitious, particularly at the start of a holiday; walk well within your capabilities.
- ☆ Allow more time than you expect to need.

The Lake District

Many guide books provide excellent summaries of the geology, history, agriculture, industry and other features which contribute to the present day appreciation of Britain's most diverse and, arguably, finest National Park. For the present purpose, it suffices to say that the southern half of the area, included in this book, has everything, and more besides, that could be desired by the country walker, with or without a pushchair.

Maps and Sketch Maps

Whilst the route directions and sketch maps should suffice for basic route finding, there is no doubt that the enjoyment of a walk is enhanced by the use of a large scale map. The Ordnance Survey Outdoor Leisure series, now incorporated into the Explorer range, retaining the previous numbers, are excellent. Sheets 6 and 7 cover the South Lakeland area.

Numbers on the sketch maps refer to instructions in the text. Start points are denoted thus: Ⓢ

Walk 1: Mickleden

Assessment: Grade 3

The route is generally level, using broad tracks and some tarmac surface. However, there is a fair amount of rough and stony surface on the outward track along Mickleden.

Distance: 4km (2½ miles)

Total ascent: Minimal

Start/car parking: National Trust pay-and-display car park by the Old Dungeon Ghyll Hotel, grid reference 286061.

Refreshments: Old Dungeon Ghyll Hotel.

Map: Ordnance Survey Explorer 6, The English Lakes, South Western area, 1:25,000.

The Area

This valley-bottom ramble is close beneath the great peaks of the Langdale Pikes, Bowfell and the Crinkle Crags. The head of Great Langdale has great landscape and historic interest, its 'U' shape determined by the scraping of the ice which laid bare the volcanic rock of the valley sides before the final retreat of the glaciers a mere 10,000 years ago. Following clearance of the original tree cover about 1,000 years ago, the pattern of land use from medieval times is clearly set out, including evidence that some land was ploughed, possibly when there was food shortage in Napoleonic times. Until comparatively recent times, the modest amount of land around the valley head was shared by no less than six farms, four of them close together by what is now Stool End Farm. The former 'intake' walls on the valley sides show the efforts made to wrest more 'improved' land from the harsh and steep terrain. At the head of this walk is the site of an early settlement, probably dating from the time when the incoming Norse settlers ('Vikings') were pushing summer grazing as high as practicable up each of the Lakeland valleys.

The Walk

Turn right from the car park to follow the roadway bearing left, behind the Old Dungeon Ghyll Hotel. In 50m, leave the tarmac at a 'path' sign, along a stony path rising to a gate. After rough cobbles the surface on this great walkers' highway to the Stake Pass and beyond improves. Go through a gate, then another in less than 50m.

The views to the left include Pike O' Blisco, Crinkle Crags, and Bowfell. Above and to the right are the Langdale Pikes, with the climbers' playground of Gimmer Crag. After the gates, the great

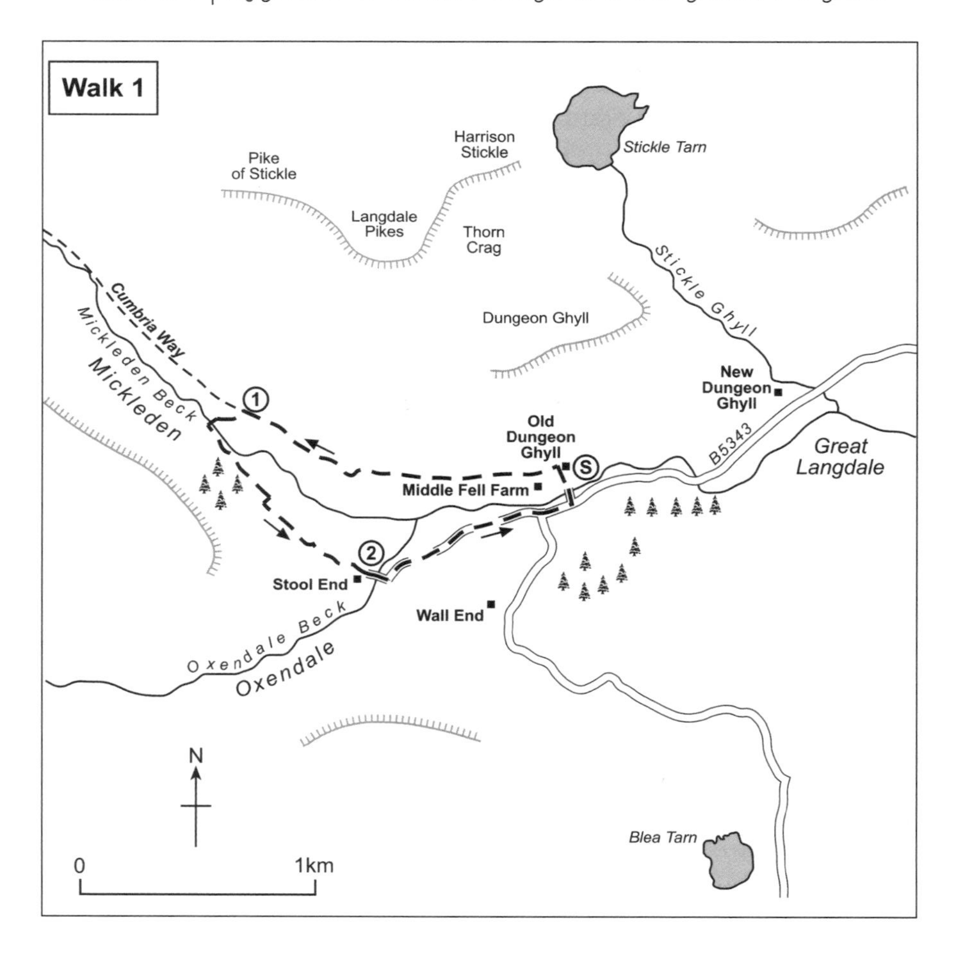

scree shoot, which was the site of a celebrated pre-historic stone axe factory, comes into view.

1. Turn left at the corner of the wall which marks the head of 'improved' land in Mickleden.

To the right is the 'Viking' settlement.

Follow a vague path over grass towards the Mickleden Beck, crossed on a footbridge, with three steps down at the far end. Bear left over grass, close to the beck, then up a slightly awkward slope to join an apparently more important track. Turn left, the track now widens with a fair surface but some standing water is possible. Cross a tiny stream. Bear right, by a 'footpath' sign, then left below a National Trust plantation. Go through a gate and continue with a wall on the left, directly to Stool End Farm. Join a major track descending from Bowfell, go through a gate and follow the 'path' sign to pass through a farm owned by the National Trust.

Middle Fell Farm

2. Leave the farm by the tarmac access road, crossing the extensive sheep pastures. Pass a cattle grid, cross Oxendale Beck, then another cattle grid, before reaching the public road at a gate. Go ahead for 50m before turning left to return to the car park.

Side Pike shows up well before the beck. As you continue, you will see a former packhorse bridge on the left, and Middle Fell Farm.

Walk 2: Elterwater and Chapel Stile

Assessment: Grade 4 (full walk) or Grade 3 (shorter walk).

Most of the total ascent occurs in the long rise from the start in Elterwater – hard work but fortunately on excellent tracks. The full walk has a section of path with rough, partially engineered, stone surface, descending quite steeply, crossing other obstacles such as little streams. Two adults would be a distinct advantage. The shorter version avoids this section.

Distance: full walk 6km (3¾ miles); shorter walk 4km (2½ miles)

Total ascent: full walk 120m (394ft); shorter walk 100m (328ft).

Start/car parking: Small National Trust car park almost opposite the Brittania Inn at Elterwater, grid reference 328048.

Refreshments: Brittania Inn, Elterwater. Brambles Tea Room, Chapel Stile.

Map: Ordnance Survey Explorer 7, The English Lakes, South Eastern area, 1:25,000.

The Area

The attractive and accessible Langdale Valley has long been a favourite with visitors of many kinds. For climbers and hill walkers, the Langdale Pikes, Bowfell and the Crinkle Crags are all close by. For the less energetic, there are routes of all kinds in the broad valley bottom and on lesser heights such as Lingmoor from which the mountain panorama can be admired. The Old Dungeon Ghyll and the New Dungeon Ghyll are hotels which, for centuries, have provided for the needs of visitors, whilst both Chapel Stile and Elterwater are charming villages. The presence of the large quarry behind Elterwater is a reminder of the extent of the industry which dominated this part of the valley, with the site of the former gunpowder works now occupied by the timeshare complex.

Chapel Stile

The Walk

Leave the car park and turn left along the public road, crossing Great Langdale Beck on the road bridge. Pass the youth hostel, then the entrance drive to the Eltermere Country House Hotel.

1. In a further 50m, turn right at a road junction to start the long rise on tarmac. Elterwater Hall is on the left. Go right at a fork, with a cul de sac sign, still on tarmac, soon rising again along a lane between stone walls, through light woodland. Ignore a track forking to the left before reaching a junction with a public bridleway on the right. Go ahead here, downhill, passing a solitary house, through Baysbrown Wood. Fortunately the trees screen most of the extensive quarry area to the right. A small, private, tarn can be seen through the trees

2. Reach Baysbrown Farm. **For the shorter version** turn right to cross the valley bottom on the farm access road, rejoining the full walk at the far end. **For the full walk**, pass the farm, rising to a gate, where the hard surface is lost. Continue along a broad, rather rough, track to Hag Wood, rising gently.

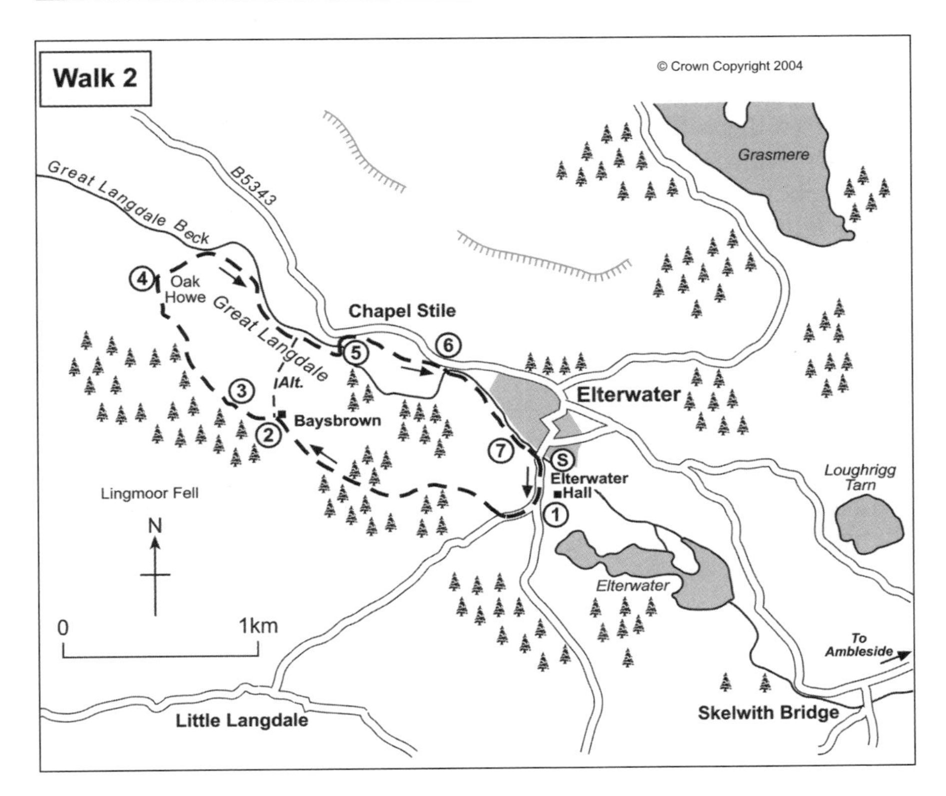

3. As the track bends to the left – 'No path' sign – fork right along 'Bridleway Gt. Langdale Dungeon Ghyll 2¾ miles', a broad stony track soon descending to cross a little stream. Go through light woodland, then into more open country with views up the valley. After passing through a gate, there are more streams and a difficult section descending steeply over rough stones, partially engineered.

4. At a waymarked junction turn right. At another waymarked junction by a stone barn turn right again to pass Oak Howe, now on a wide, easy track across the valley bottom, with fine views of the Langdale Pikes. Bear right, through a gate, ignoring the footbridge on the left. Continue alongside the raised bank of the Great Langdale Beck. The shorter route joins from the right. Go through a gate by a cattle grid.

5. Bear left through a gate by a cattle grid and cross the beck at New Bridge. Follow a wide unsurfaced road heading towards Chapel Stile village. Before reaching the valley road, fork right, along a narrower track between stone walls. Go through a little gate to reach tarmac then turn left through a gate, passing the tiny hamlet based on Thrang Farm. At a junction, go right, then left in a further 20m ('footpath' sign on wall), before bearing left to descend to the public road.

Chapel Stile village, with store and café is to the left. Public conveniences are opposite.

6. Turn right, along the roadside, past Wainwrights Inn. At the far end of the car parking area, turn right ('public bridleway' sign) to cross the beck on a wooden footbridge. Turn right at the far end, then bear left around the base of a little knoll. Stay with the fine path along the foot of the great spoil heaps, with the Langdale timeshare in view across the beck. Rise quite steeply over a stony section to join the tarmac surfaced quarry access road. Turn left to walk downhill back to Elterwater.

Walk 3: Grasmere and Easedale

Assessment: Grade 2

An easy little walk with a small amount of ascent. There is also a footbridge with steps at either end, followed by a short section of rough-surfaced track.

Distance: 2.7km (1¾ miles).

Total ascent: 20m (66ft).

Start/car parking: Use any car park in the village centre.

Refreshments: Selection of inns and cafés in Grasmere.

Map: Ordnance Survey Explorer 7, The English Lakes, South Eastern area, 1:25,000.

Grasmere and Helm Crag

The Area

The well-known village of Grasmere is well provided with shops and other attractions for visitors, including Wordsworth connections, the parish church and the gingerbread shop. This route explores the area between the village and the prominent peak of Helm Crag.

The Walk

From any car park walk to the road junction by the book shop. Turn into Easedale Road, opposite. Part way along the road, go left through a gate, then right to follow a well-surfaced National Trust permissive path beside the road. Ahead, there are views up the Easedale Valley. At the far end, go through a gate to rejoin the road, soon crossing Easedale Beck at Goody Bridge.

1. At a road junction in a further 50m, go straight ahead to reach a footbridge on the left, with steps at each end – this is a good picnic area. Cross the bridge and continue along a path engineered with uncomfortably large stones. There is an 'Easedale Tarn' signpost. Go through a gate, with the Easedale waterfalls in view ahead and Helm Crag to the right.

   The surface improves before a wall on the left is reached. Turn right to cross New Bridge over Easedale Beck, continue over grass, cross a tiny stream and go through a gate into a narrow walled lane. Go through a gate to a tarmac surfaced road at a hamlet.

2. Turn right to follow a roadway across a field, with Stone Arthur above, to the left. Turn left in 150m, before the house 'Helm End'. The track is initially tarmac surfaced, soon lost as it rises gently. Cross the Lancrigg access drive and continue to rise past Thorney How youth hostel to reach a junction with a very minor road.

   In view are the Travellers' Rest Inn, Seat Sandal, Great Rigg and Fairfield.

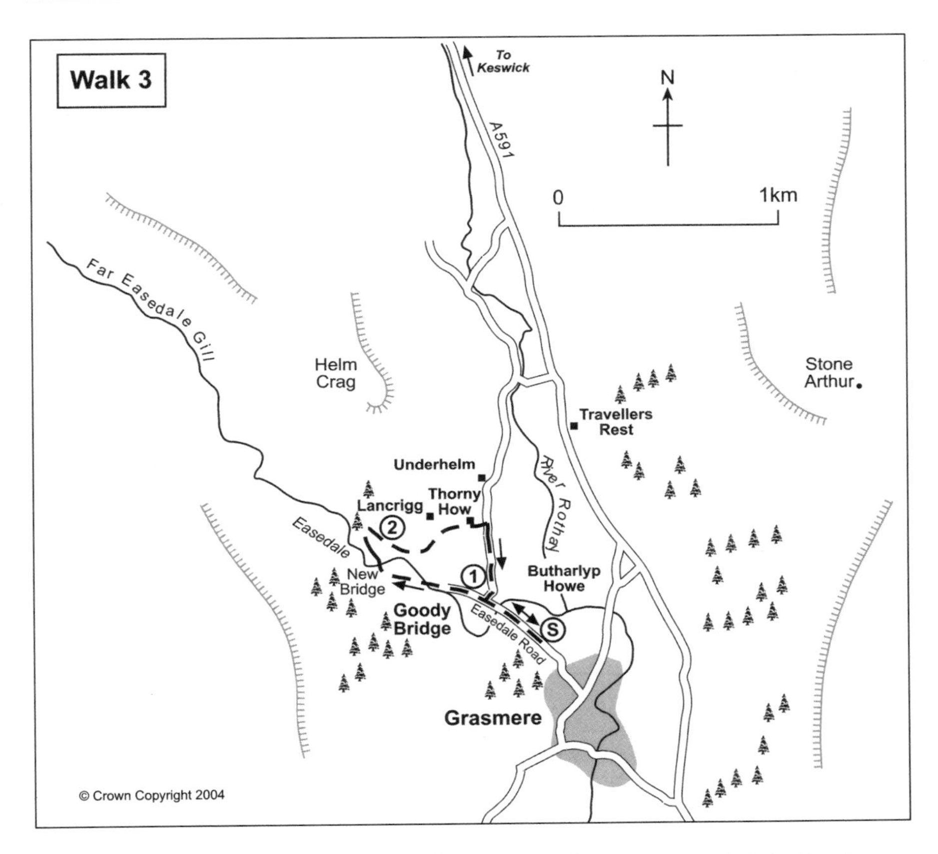

Turn right, soon rejoining the outward route at point 1, the junction above Goody Bridge. Turn left to return to the car park.

Walk 4: Grasmere Village and Butharlyp Howe

Assessment: Grade 2

Basically a short, easy walk on good surfaces, level apart from the short rise behind Butharlyp Howe. No stiles or difficult gates.

Distance: 3km (1¾ miles).

Total ascent: 25m (82ft).

Start/car parking: Layby on the east side of the A591 main road, approximately 400m north of the mini roundabout at the village access, grid reference 342075.

Refreshments: Inns and cafés in Grasmere.

Map: Ordnance Survey Explorer 7, The English Lakes, South Eastern area, 1:25,000.

The Area

This circuit combines the riverside path behind much of the Grasmere village centre, crossing the River Rothay on the relatively new Millennium Bridge, with the rising track behind the knoll of Butharlyp Howe. The return is through the village centre, with the Heaton Cooper studio, Sara Nelson's gingerbread shop and St Oswald's parish church (Wordsworth is buried in the churchyard) all en route.

The Walk

Cross the A591 to a gate, then follow a good track to a junction in about 200m.

1. Go ahead at the junction, crossing the Millennium Bridge over the River Rothay; there is a plaque on a boulder at the far side

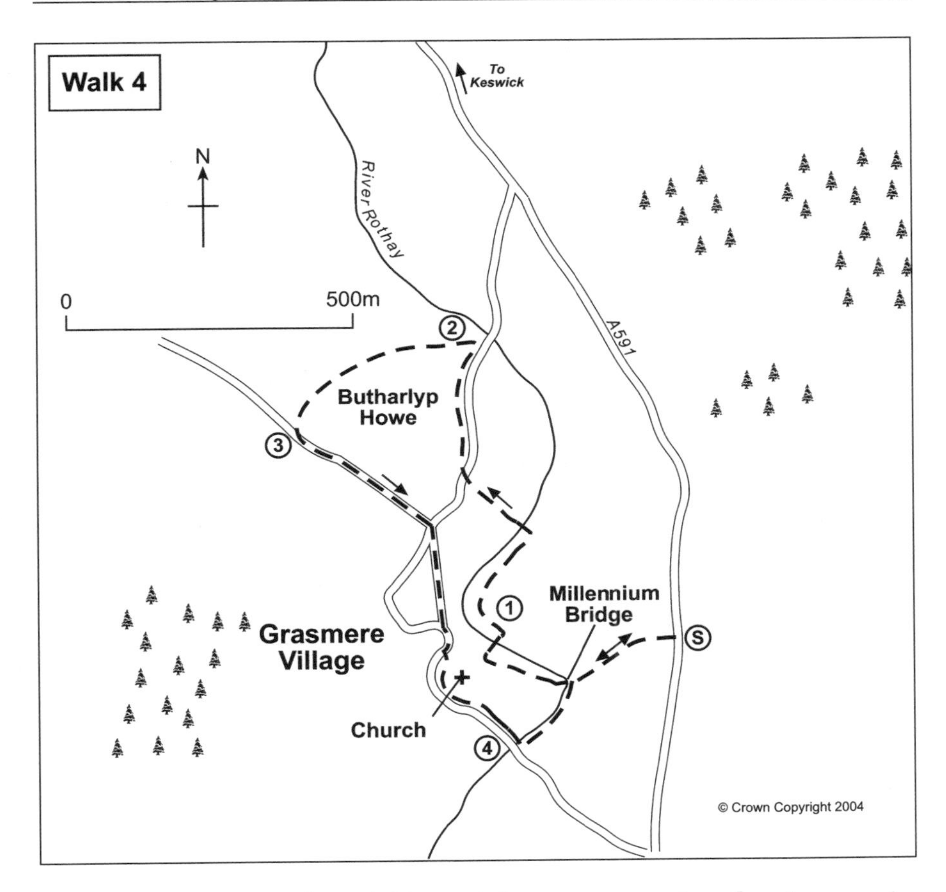

and a sign 'Broadgate'. Turn right, soon crossing the river again on a footbridge with good views of the sharp little peak of Helm Crag. Go straight across an unmade road and continue to another bridge over the river, leading into a car park close to the village hall, where there is a children's play area to the right. Turn right to walk along the roadside for almost 300m.

2. Immediately before the road rises to cross the river, turn left at a gate signposted 'National Trust Butharlyp Howe' to follow a wide track in woodland, soon narrowing and rising quite steeply for a short distance, above the river. Go through a gate at the side of Silver Lea guest house to join the Easedale Road.

The Millennium Bridge, Grasmere

3. Turn left to walk by the roadside to the village centre, passing the village green (and public conveniences), then the Wordsworth Hotel, the gingerbread shop and the church.

4. From the church retrace the route as far as a path on the right leading past the Wordsworth Memorial Garden to the Millenium Bridge. Cross the brige to rejoin the outward route and return to the main road and the car park.

Walk 5: Grasmere and Rydal

Assessment: Grade 5

This arises from a combination of length, awkward footbridge and difficult track on the 'coffin route'. Two adults required.

Distance: 7.7km (4¾ miles).

Total ascent: 180m (591ft).

Start/car parking: National Trust pay-and-display car park, with public conveniences, at White Moss Common, by the (river) side of the A591, grid reference 350065.

Refreshments: Short deviation to tea shop behind Rydal Hall.

Map: Ordnance Survey Explorer 7, The English Lakes, South Eastern area, 1:25,000.

The Area

This route traverses an immensely popular area, including White Moss, the shore of the lovely Grasmere, Loughrigg Terrace, Rydal caves, Rydal church, Rydal Hall, Rydal Mount and the 'coffin road'. The views throughout are splendid and the necessary effort is well rewarded.

The Walk

From the car park, start along the broad track, with the river to the left, crossing a stream on a broad wooden bridge, through light woodland. Reach a junction, with a footbridge on the left. Do not cross; go through the gate on the right and continue along the edge of a field, with the river on the left. Go through a gate and rise through woodland. There are a few awkward stones, before the end of a long footbridge across the river is reached. At deck level, this bridge is only 56cm (less than 2ft!) in width but the sides are tapered, making

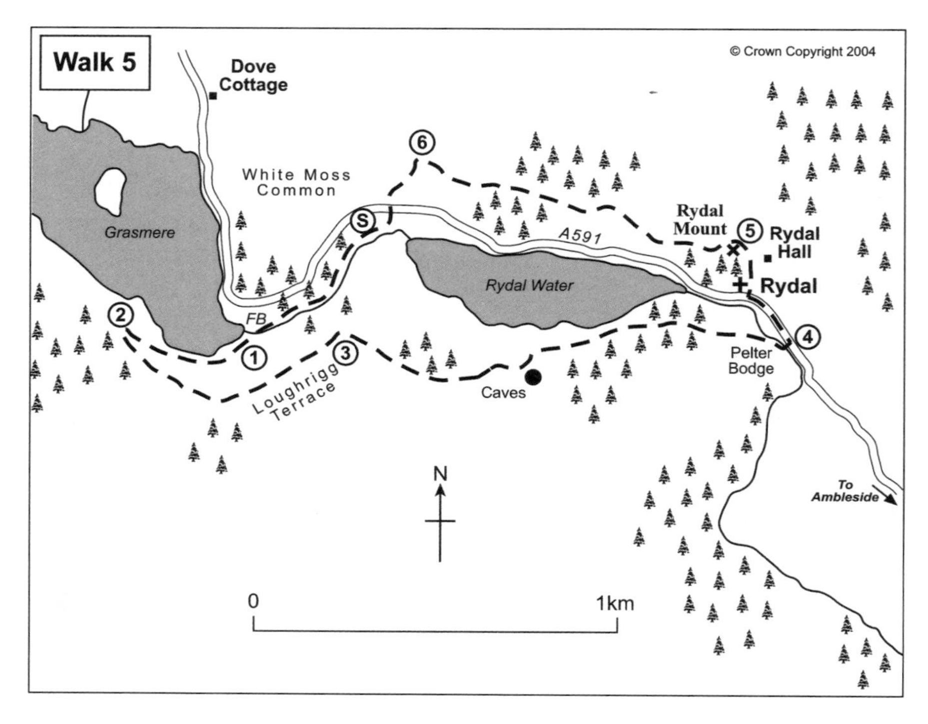

crossing possible for many ATP's by forward tilting; otherwise folding is required.

1. Cross the bridge then turn right to pass the end of a weir and along part of the Grasmere shore – a wonderful picnic spot. An awkward little slope can be avoided on grass to the left. At the far end of the shingle beach go through a gate then fork left in 40m to follow a good track, uphill through the woods. In 100m, fork left to continue rising, soon reaching Deerbolts Lodge, with the public road a little further.

2. Turn sharp left in front of the lodge, by a National Trust 'Deerbolts Wood' sign. A fine, broad, track rises gently through the wood. Go through the gate at the top 'High Close'. Join another track, bearing left, downhill to another gate and a sign 'Loughrigg Fell'. There is a short awkward section, then the delectable Loughrigg Terrace, with the ultimate 'picturesque'

The view from Loughrigg Terrace

landscape and seats to savour the views of the lake and fells including Helm Crag and much of the Fairfield Horseshoe. At a fork, keep left to stay with the main rack.

3. At a junction at the far end of the terrace turn right, down a rocky section. Turn right again in 100m., rising a little to follow another terraced path, the views now including Rydal Water. Reach a stony area with cairn and the great Rydal Cave. The track now loops to descend through woodland as a rough stony path. Go through a gate and rise gently above the woodland. After another gate, the roadway is tarmac surfaced, passing a terrace of cottages before descending past a small car park and a cattle grid to a road junction. Turn left to cross the road bridge over the River Rothay and join the A591.

4. Turn left along the roadside footpath for about 200m. Cross the road and turn right towards 'Rydal Mount', rising quite steeply up the little cul de sac road. Pass Rydal church and the entrance to Rydal Hall – a short diversion to the right at the second access

leads to a tea shop behind the hall. Pass the entrance to Rydal Mount for a steep little push (right or left) to a junction.

5. Turn left for 'Harthead Barn' and 'public bridleway Grasmere' This is the well-known 'coffin road'. Pass above Rydal Mount, then through a waymarked gate in less than 50m., then another gate to follow a rough-surfaced path descending gently under the steep lower slopes of Nab Scar. The views are of Loughrigg, over Rydal Water. Rise to a gate, pass through a gateway, then two more gates before reaching a section with awkward stones, followed by a difficult length of path with many obstructive tree roots. A choice may be made between staying close to the wall on the left or going straight ahead. Neither route is ideal for an ATP and there are also channels across the path. After 100m or so, the path improves. Go through a little gate.

6. About 30m after the gate turn left at a junction; there is a cottage above to the right. Descend quite steeply beside a little stream, the path being initially narrow but widening after a gateway part-way down. Cross the stream; there is a waterfall to the right. Continue, to reach the A591, crossing the road to return to the lower car park.

Walk 6: Ambleside and High Sweden Bridge

Assessment: Grade 4

A long ascent, coupled with significant sections of rough stony track. No stiles or awkward gates.

Distance: 5km (3 miles), out and back.

Total ascent: 200m (656ft).

Start/car parking: Main car park in Rydal Road, Ambleside, grid reference 375047.

Refreshments: Wide choice of inns and cafés in Ambleside.

Map: Ordnance Survey Explorer 7, The English Lake District, South Eastern area, 1:25,000.

The Area

High Sweden bridge has long been a favourite destination for ramblers, readily reached from Ambleside by a straightforward track. The lovely former packhorse bridge spans the Scandale Beck in a broad valley above the town. Those without pushchairs can continue on the far side of the bridge, circling back to Ambleside via Low Sweden Bridge. Although the great majority of this return route is on a good track, the section immediately after High Sweden Bridge climbs quite steeply along a narrow, difficult, path and cannot be recommended for the present purpose.

The Walk

From the main car park, turn right for a short distance, cross the road by the mini roundabout, and continue steeply up Smithy Brow, soon passing the turning to Nook Lane.

1. Turn left along Sweden Bridge Lane and follow this residential

High Sweden Bridge

lane for some distance. At a road junction go straight ahead at a 'to Sweden Bridge' sign. At the top of the hard-surfaced lane go through a gate.

2. The broad track continues, with very variable surface, including rough sections, soon descending a little before continuing the steady rise.

The mountain views over the wall on the left are splendid.

Go through a gate and enter light woodland before passing two long defunct former quarries. The track is very much along the side of the Scandale valley, with the beck rushing and tumbling over rapids and little falls below. Go through another gate and continue, soon reaching the exposed rock over which the bridge is reached on the left in a few metres

3. High Sweden Bridge must be one of the finest (and most popular) picnic sites in the whole of the Lake District.

Return to Ambleside by the same route.

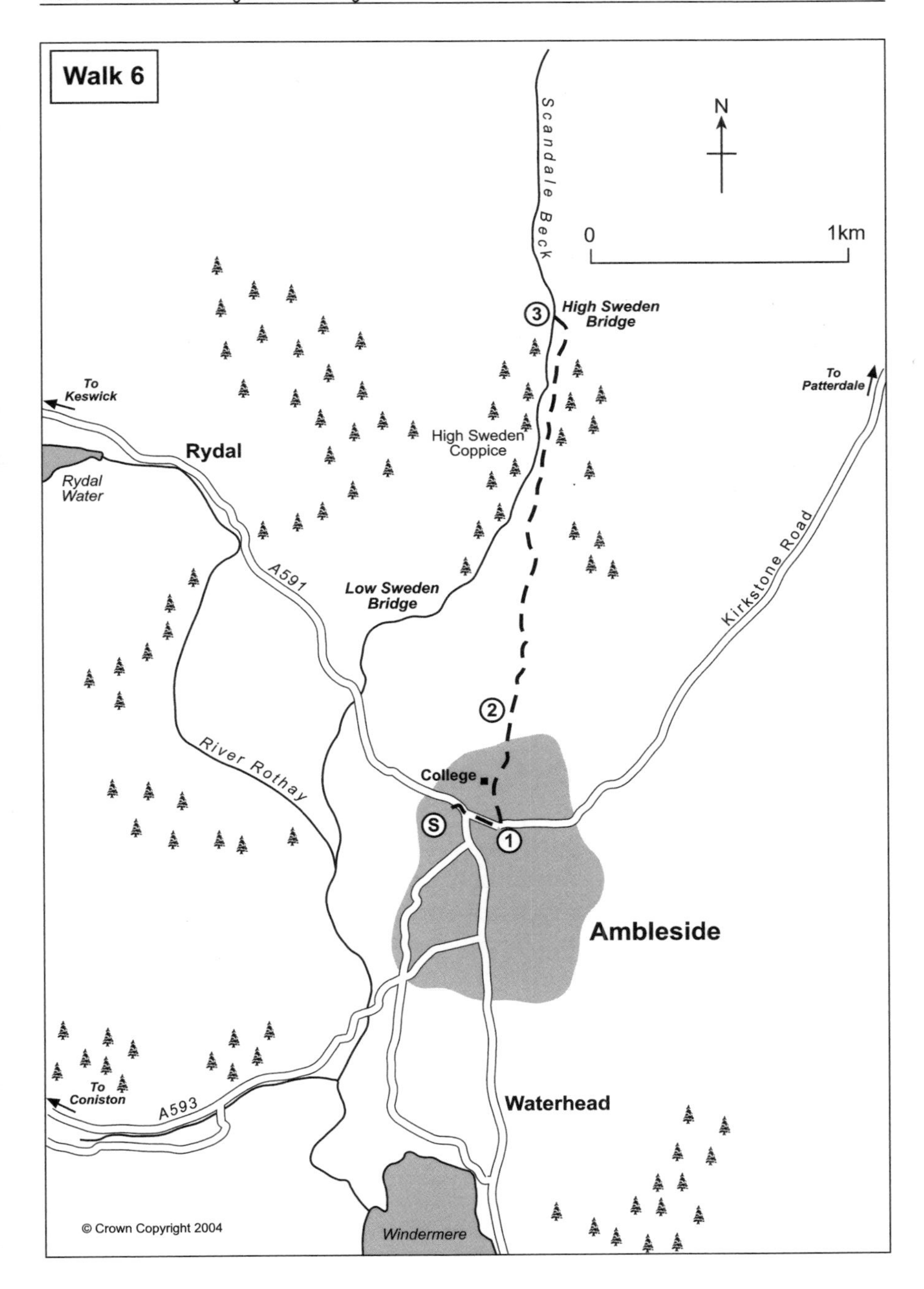
Walk 6
N
0
1km
Scandale Beck
High Sweden Bridge
To Keswick
To Patterdale
Rydal
Rydal Water
High Sweden Coppice
A591
Low Sweden Bridge
Kirkstone Road
River Rothay
College
Ambleside
To Coniston
A593
Waterhead
Windermere
© Crown Copyright 2004

Walk 7: Ambleside and Stock Ghyll

Assessment: Grade 4

A long uphill push but few problems underfoot. The suggested diversion to include the path by the waterfalls adds steps and other difficulties, making the circuit **Grade 5**, with two adults required.

Distance: 4km (2½ miles).

Total ascent: 160m (525ft).

Start/car parking: Main car park in Ambleside, to the north of the village centre, grid reference 375047.

Refreshments: Wide choice in Ambleside.

Map: Ordnance Survey Explorer 7, The English Lakes, South Eastern area, 1:25,000.

The Area

This circuit rises along the side of the valley with Stock Ghyll and its famous waterfalls, crossing the Ghyll further upstream before returning to Ambleside, partially along the Kirkstone road. As parts of this road are narrow, this walk is probably better avoided at peak holiday times. The oldest part of Ambleside (16th century), below the former St Anne's church, is traversed before the return to the car park.

The centre of Ambleside has a good array of mainly harmonious Victorian buildings, many of them now shops and cafés. The village (town?) is famed for the number and diversity of its retailers of outdoor clothing (the 'anorak capital of Britain'!).

The Walk

From the car park, walk back to the village centre, passing the Tourist Information Centre.

1. Turn left immediately after passing the Salutation Hotel, an old coaching inn. Turn left again in a few metres to commence the long ascent of tarmac-surfaced Stock Ghyll Lane. (There are a few car parking spaces beside the wall on the right, use of which would avoid the car park charges, but the disc parking scheme does limit waiting to a maximum of 1 hour.) Rise steadily with the waters of the Ghyll, which formerly powered several mills in this area, to the left. Pass a modern residential development on the right to reach a junction in a further 40m.

2. **For the diversion**, turn left here 'to the Waterfalls'. Go through a gate to follow a path through the woodland, soon rising steeply, with rough stone and tree roots. There are red waymarks and occasional seats and picnic tables. Negotiate a flight of steps, leading to a viewing platform for the falls. Continue, up more steps, to a junction. Turn right, heading for a 'revolving gate' and leave the falls area through a gate beside the (possibly Victorian) turnstile. Rejoin the road, turning left up the hill.

   Without the diversion, carry on along the road, rising steeply to pass another residential development, then a cattle grid leading into open countryside.

3. Continue along the private roadway to Grove Farm.

   The views to the left are of the long south ridge of Red Screes.

   Pass 'Mountain View', then a cattle grid and a dilapidated barn. Cross a little stream, pass Low Grove House and another cattle grid.

4. Turn left immediately to leave the roadway along a waymarked path down the valley side. Go through a gate at the bottom and cross the Ghyll on a bridge. Carry on along a narrower path with the Ghyll on the left, soon looping up the valley side. The views are now of Wansfell Pike. Go through a gate at the top to reach Roundhill Farm. There is a 'footpath' sign on a wall. In 25m, turn

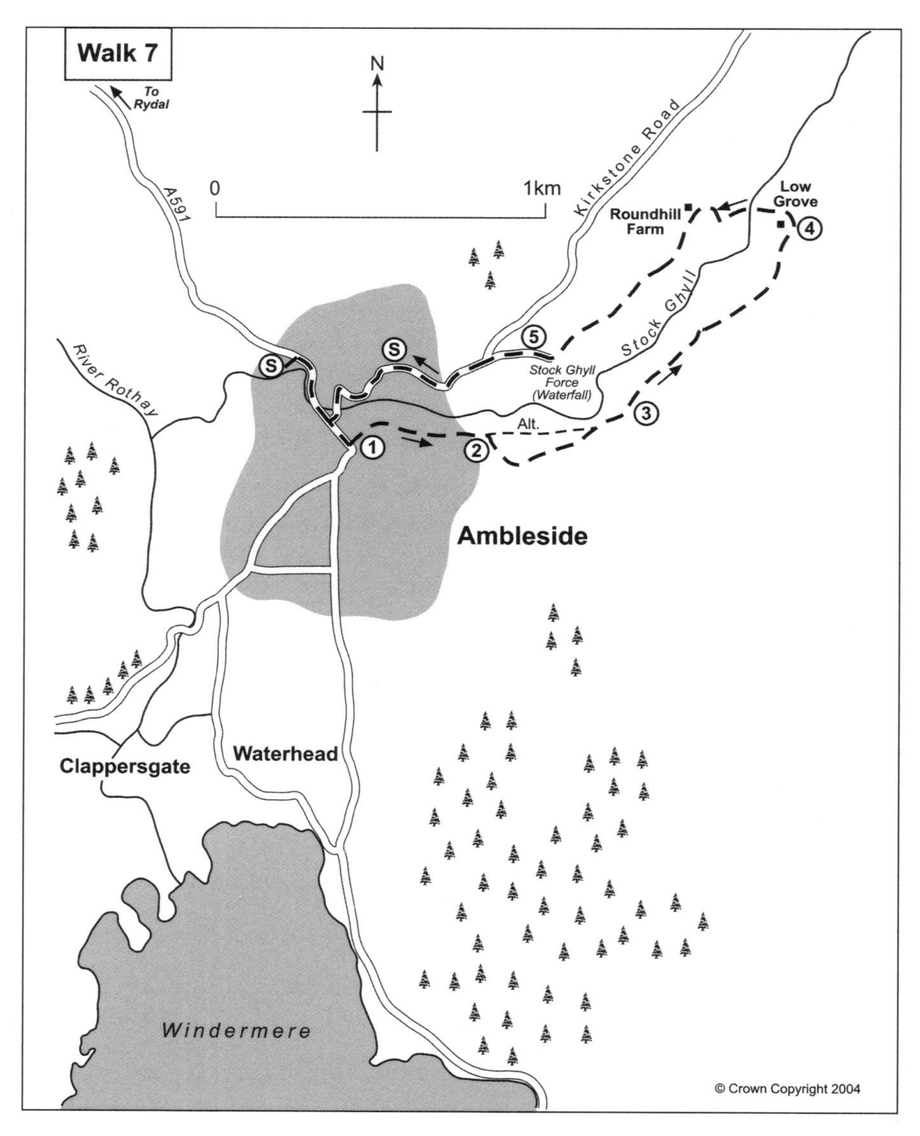

left through a farm gate to descend a muddy, cattle-churned track across a field for 100m. After another gate, there is a short rise before continuing the descent towards Ambleside, with a wall on the left.

Ambleside, above Peggy Hill

The views are superb – the Coniston Fells, with Wetherlam prominent ahead, and the Crinkle Crags and Bowfell further to the right.

Continue ahead, soon approaching a house. Go through two gates before reaching a little tarmac-surfaced lane. Pass through Seathwaite hamlet bearing right to join the Kirkstone road.

5. Turn left to commence the descent to Ambleside, taking great care on the narrow sections before the roadside pavement is reached. Immediately before the former St Anne's church, where a small board by the entrance has historic information, turn left into 'Fairview Road leading to Peggy Hill'. Pass behind Ambleside's oldest house (part is the 'Old School House') which has some fine Lakeland chimneys, to reach the top of Peggy Hill. Descend to North Road, turning left to the Tourist Information Office and a choice of refreshment opportunities. Turn right at the main street to return to the car park

Walk 8: Ambleside and Rydal

Assessment: Grade 2

A level ramble on minor roads and first-rate tracks. Grade 2 only because of the distance.

Distance: 5.5km (3½ miles).

Total ascent: negligible.

Start/car parking: Main public car park in Ambleside, Rydal Road, grid reference 376047.

Refreshments: Wide choice in Ambleside. Tea room behind Rydal Hall.

Map: Ordnance Survey Explorer 7, the English Lakes, South Eastern area, 1:25,000.

The Area

This circuit links the immensely popular town of Ambleside with the hamlet of Rydal, where Rydal Hall, Rydal Mount and Rydal Church all add to the attraction for visitors. Although the route is entirely within a very civilised valley, there are good mountain views.

Despite the large numbers of visitors, Ambleside remains a fine little town, with many shops (particularly those selling outdoor clothing!), inns and cafés. The Armitt is an interesting small museum/gallery close to the car park.

Rydal is most famous for the William Wordsworth connections. The poet lived at Rydal Mount from 1813 until his death in 1850. The house is open to the public for most of the year. During this time the owner of Rydal Hall, Lady Diana le Fleming paid for the construction of Rydal Church, which has since been enlarged (Wordsworth complained that the original was too small). Inside the church are the pews used by Wordsworth and by Dr Arnold, the headmaster of Rugby school who had a house built (with Wordsworth's advice) at Fox How across the river. Behind the church is Dora's field, purchased by Wordsworth when he believed that eviction from Rydal Mount, which he rented from Lady le Fleming, was likely. He intended to build a house on this site. The field, which has splendid daffodils, is named after his daughter.

Rydal Hall is used as a retreat centre by the Diocese of Carlisle. The hall itself is not open to the public – but there seems to be no objection to passers-by having a discreet peep at the Rydal Falls. Also, the gardens are open to the public (donation box in aid of restoration) and there is a tea shop.

Rydal Hall

The Walk

From the car park, turn left along the main road, towards Grasmere. Fortunately, there is a roadside footpath. Opposite the car park exit are the attractive buildings of the Charlotte Mason campus of University of Cumbria. The original building was the home of the celebrated Harriet Martineau.

1. Shortly after crossing Scandale Beck, cross the road to an obvious lodge, with iron gates and a 'Rydal Hall' footpath sign. Follow the broad track rising gently through the parkland for about 1.5km (1 mile) to the hall.

Ahead is Nab Scar, with the ridge of Heron Pike and Great Rigg leading the eye towards Fairfield, the summit of the well-known

'Horseshoe' walk. Across the valley is the bulk of Loughrigg, with Crinkle Crags and Bowfell peeping through the gap above Red Bank.

As the hall is approached, the track passes through light woodland, with some good specimen trees.

2. At a junction close to the hall, the signposted path turns right, uphill.

A short, permissive, diversion through a gate to the left gives access to a bridge over Rydal Beck, with a fine view of the lower Rydal waterfall, much admired by Constable, Turner and other painters. Immediately below is a little building dating from 1669, one of the first 'viewing houses' in the country, with its only window facing the fall, providing a framed picture of great charm. Beyond the bridge are blocks of stone sculpted by the celebrated local sculptress, Josefina de Vasconcellos and her students.

Return to the path, passing through the outbuildings of the hall, including the Bulley Barn and a youth centre. Close to the latter building is sited a turbine which provides electricity for all the buildings on the site. Go round the rear of the hall, its oldest part, then pass the café before reaching the road a little way below Rydal Mount.

3. Turn left to descend to the main road, passing Rydal church. Turn left to follow the main road for a short distance, then turn right, over Pelter Bridge, to take a minor road across the water meadows. Accompanied by the River Rothay, this quiet road provides a good walking route, undulating pleasantly around the foot of Loughrigg, with views of Wansfell Pike over Ambleside town and of the ridge which leads over Snarker Pike to Red Screes. On the left is Fox How, 19th-century home of Dr Arnold.

4. After about 2km (1¼ miles) turn left to cross the river on an elegant former packhorse bridge. **Either** go straight ahead to return directly to the car park **or** fork right to cross Stock Ghyll

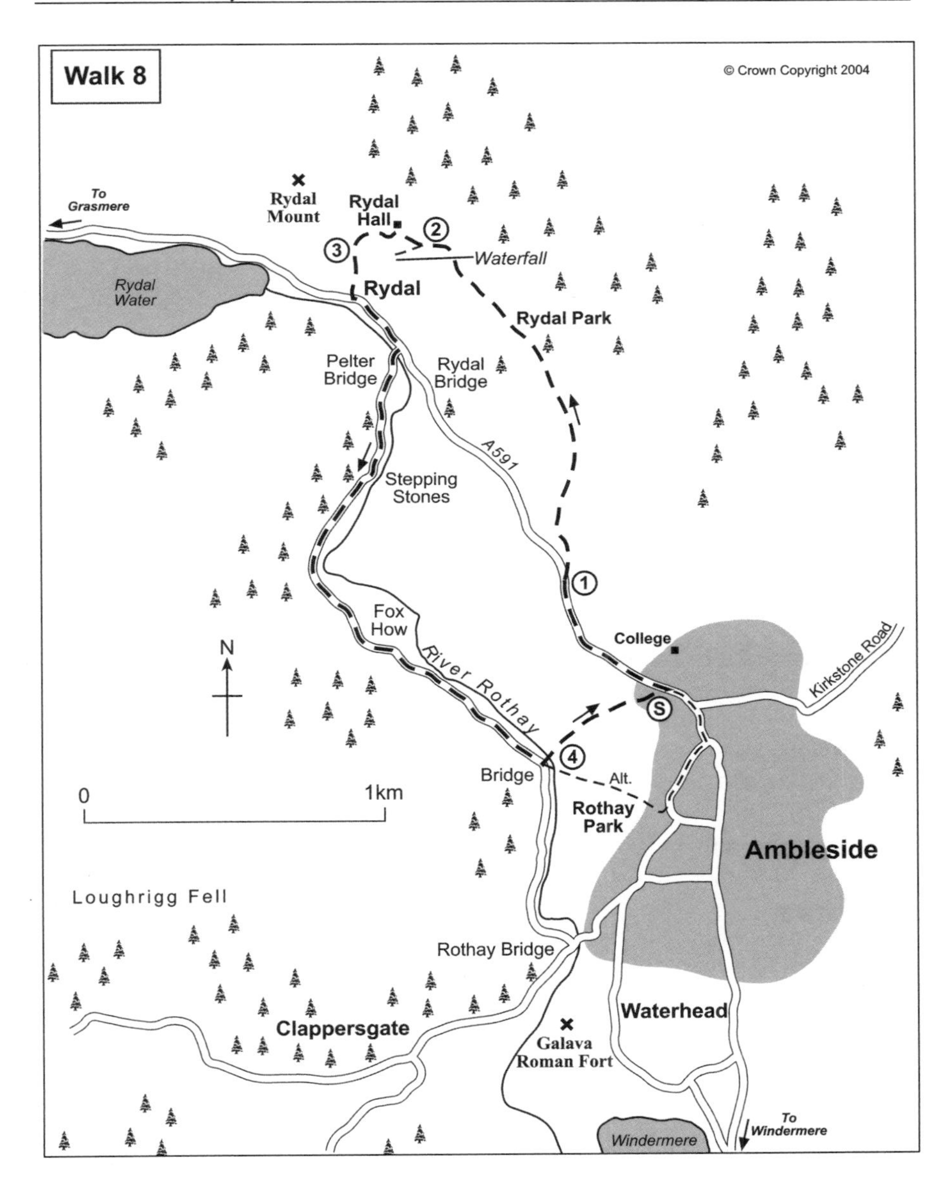

Beck and continue across Rothay Park to reach Ambleside by the Victorian parish church. Walk through the town, bearing left to return to the car park.

Walk 9: Loughrigg Tarn

Assessment: Grade 1

A short, mainly level, ramble on good tracks and a minor road.

Distance: 2.5km (1½ miles).

Total ascent: 20m (66ft).

Start/car parking: Small off-road area 30m along the little road which leads to the entrance to the Neaum Crag chalet site, grid reference 346040. Easily reached from the road connecting Ambleside with Skelwith Bridge. Turn right towards Red Bank and Grasmere.

Refreshments: In season, Oaks Farm serves a variety of light refreshments.

Map: Ordnance Survey Explorer 7, The English Lakes, South Eastern area, 1:25,000

The Area

At the foot of the steep slopes of Loughrigg, the tarn has a pretty situation, providing an attractive focus for this gentle circular route.

The Walk

Turn right from the parking area, back to the junction in 30m. Turn right, cross the stream on the road bridge, then turn left in 40m to rise gently along a tarmac surfaced roadway. Turn right, in front of cottages, as the surface roughens. At a junction in 60m, bear left through a gate with a 'Loughrigg Tarn and Grasmere' sign to follow a

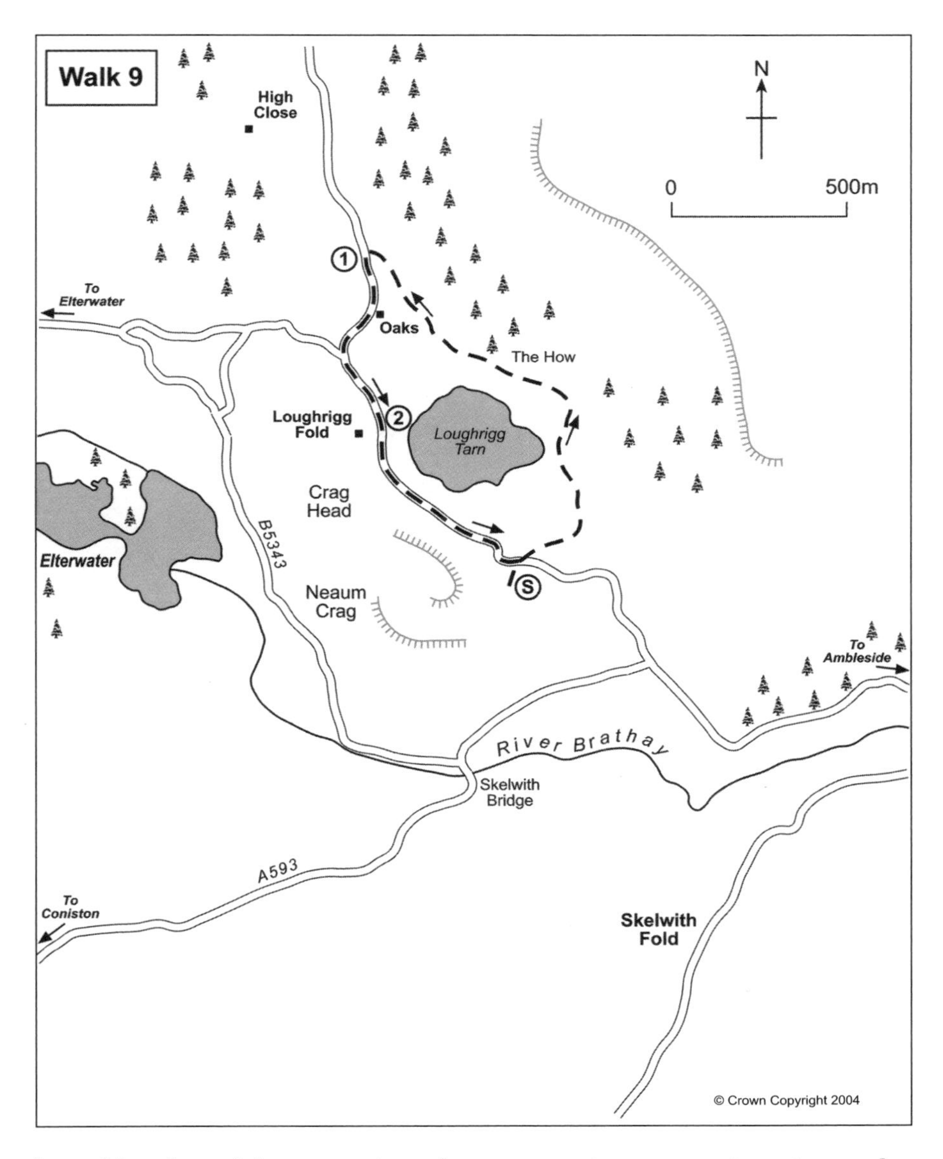

broad level track between iron fences, passing a camping site on the left. Loughrigg is close on the right, with the summit in view. The tarn is soon visible. Pass The How, house and bank barn. Go through a gate, to join the public road.

1. Turn left. Pass Oaks, an old farmstead with bank barns. Turn left at a road junction for 'Ambleside, Coniston'.

2. At the crest of the rise, for the standard circuit continue along the roadside as far as the original junction. Turn right to reach the car park in 30m.

Near Loughrigg Tarn

Walk 10: Elterwater and Skelwith Bridge

Assessment: Grade 3; the shorter version is Grade 1.

Basically this is a very easy walk, short, flat and with a good surface on the great majority of the track. However, close to the waterfall there is a length of path which is narrow, with difficult projecting stones and tree roots. For this section only, the presence of two adults would be a distinct advantage.

Distance: 4.5km (2¾ miles). A shorter version, avoiding the awkward section of path, gives a walk of about 3km (2¼ miles).

Total ascent: Negligible.

Start/car parking: Small National Trust car park almost opposite the Brittania Inn, Elterwater, grid reference 328048.

Refreshments: Brittania Inn, Elterwater. Kirkstone Gallery, Skelwith Bridge.

Map: O.S Explorer 7, The English Lakes, South Eastern area, 1:25,000.

The Area

The route follows the bottom of the lovely Langdale Valley through woods and meadows, broad and gentle, never far from the Great Langdale Beck/River Brathay, passing the shore of Elterwater. In view are the magnificent Langdale Pikes, Lingmoor and Silver How. At one end is the charming hamlet of Elterwater; at the other end Skelwith Bridge includes a slate dressing factory, the Skelwith Bridge Hotel and the Kirkstone Gallery complex, with its tea room. Close to Skelwith Bridge, Skelwith Force makes up in sheer power for its modest height as a waterfall.

The Langdale Pikes, viewed from the walk

The Walk

1. Leave the car park through the gate to follow an artificially surfaced path beside the river. The path soon loses its surface but remains entirely easy to follow. Go through a gate before entering woodland, a low-lying area of lake-edge swamp. Pass along the edge of the lake, a superb picnic/children's play place, before entering woodland again.

   The track becomes rougher as it passes above the waterfall, reached by a very short (non-pushchair) diversion. Continue, soon passing through part of the old slate works before reaching the Kirkstone Gallery.

2. Just a little further is another excellent waterside picnic/play area.

   Return to Elterwater by the same route.

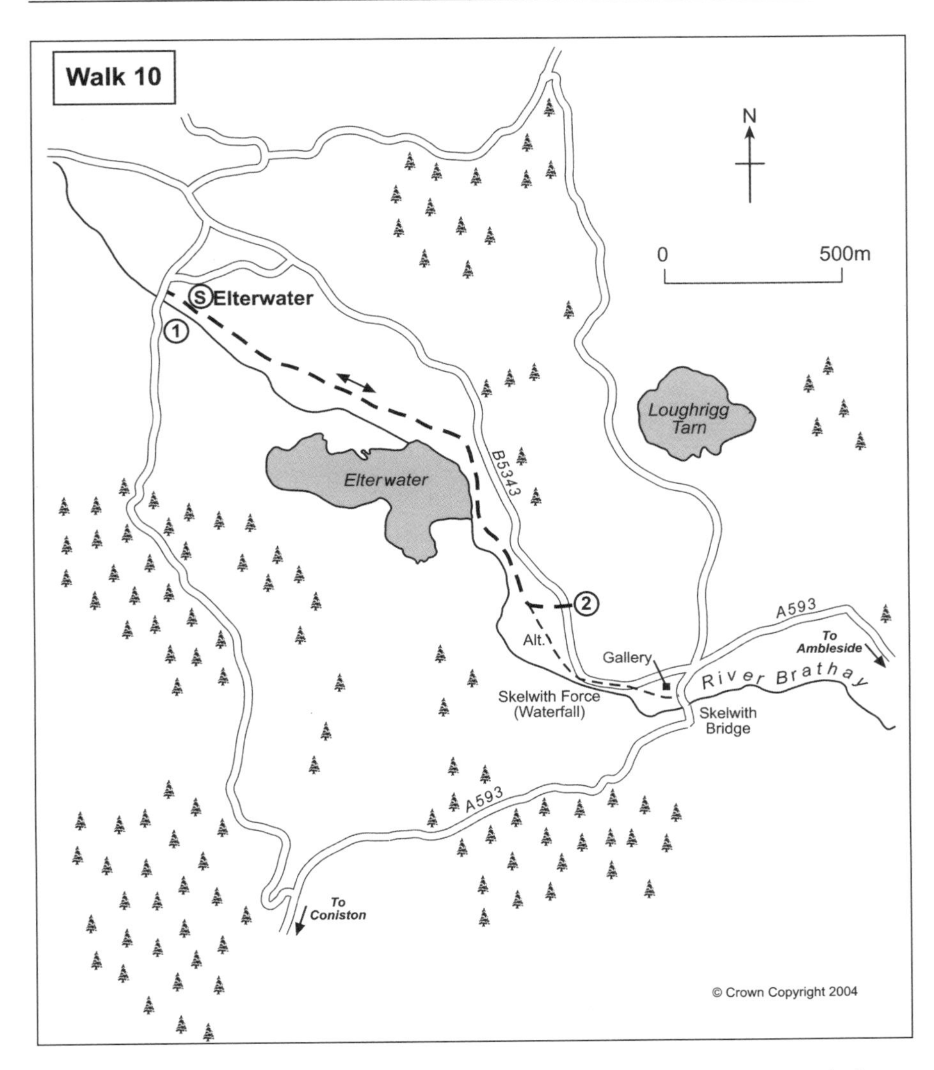

The shorter walk is best started at the Skelwith Bridge end, from the car park on the Langdale road which is situated on the right, less than half a mile after the road junction at Skelwith Bridge, grid reference 341037. Cross the road to a gate almost opposite the car park, then follow the recently made path down to a footbridge and gate. Continue along the path in the same direction for a short distance to join the main path described above. Turn right to walk to Elterwater. Return by the same route.

To visit the waterfall, a diversion to the left on joining the main path is required. This diversion necessitates using some of the awkward section of footpath.

Walk 11: Tarn Hows

Assessment: Grade 1

A broad, easy track, with modest rise and fall and no steep gradients. A lovely circuit with or without an ATP.

Distance: 3.2km (2 miles).

Total ascent: 60m (197ft).

Start/car parking: National Trust car park, grid reference 325995. The access road, signposted, leaves the Hawkshead to Coniston road close to Hawkshead Hill hamlet.

Refreshments: None. Drive to Hawkshead or Coniston.

Map: Ordnance Survey Explorer 7, The English Lakes, South Eastern area, 1:25,000.

Tarn Hows

The Area

A fine example of the more gentle type of Lakeland scenery, but with the big mountains never far away. Surprisingly, this is a man-made landscape, the tarn being the result of damming a marshy valley to provide water power for a sawmill. The tree plantations – oak, rowan, larch, pine and spruce have matured well to provide the perfect setting for the tarn.

The Walk

Leave the car park through the gate. Cross the public road, pass a vehicular barrier and go down a broad, easy, track towards the tarn. Bear to the left then fork right to continue the descent.

1. Go through a gate and cross over the outlet stream. Continue through the light woodland along the shore of the tarn, crossing another stream. Keep right at a fork with mini signpost before rising moderately steeply. There are occasional seats by the side of the track. At a junction with signpost, follow 'Hawkshead around tarn'.

2. Go through a gate to reach the head of the tarn and a little bridge.

   Black Crag is the modest peak visible to the left.

   Continue, rising steadily at a gentle gradient. At a junction go straight ahead, signposted 'Coniston Yewdale', soon crossing open hillside, with the best views of the tarn and its islands. There are abundant waterside picnic/play sites. Cross a stream, go through a gate and rise towards the public road. Join the road, bearing right to return to the car park.

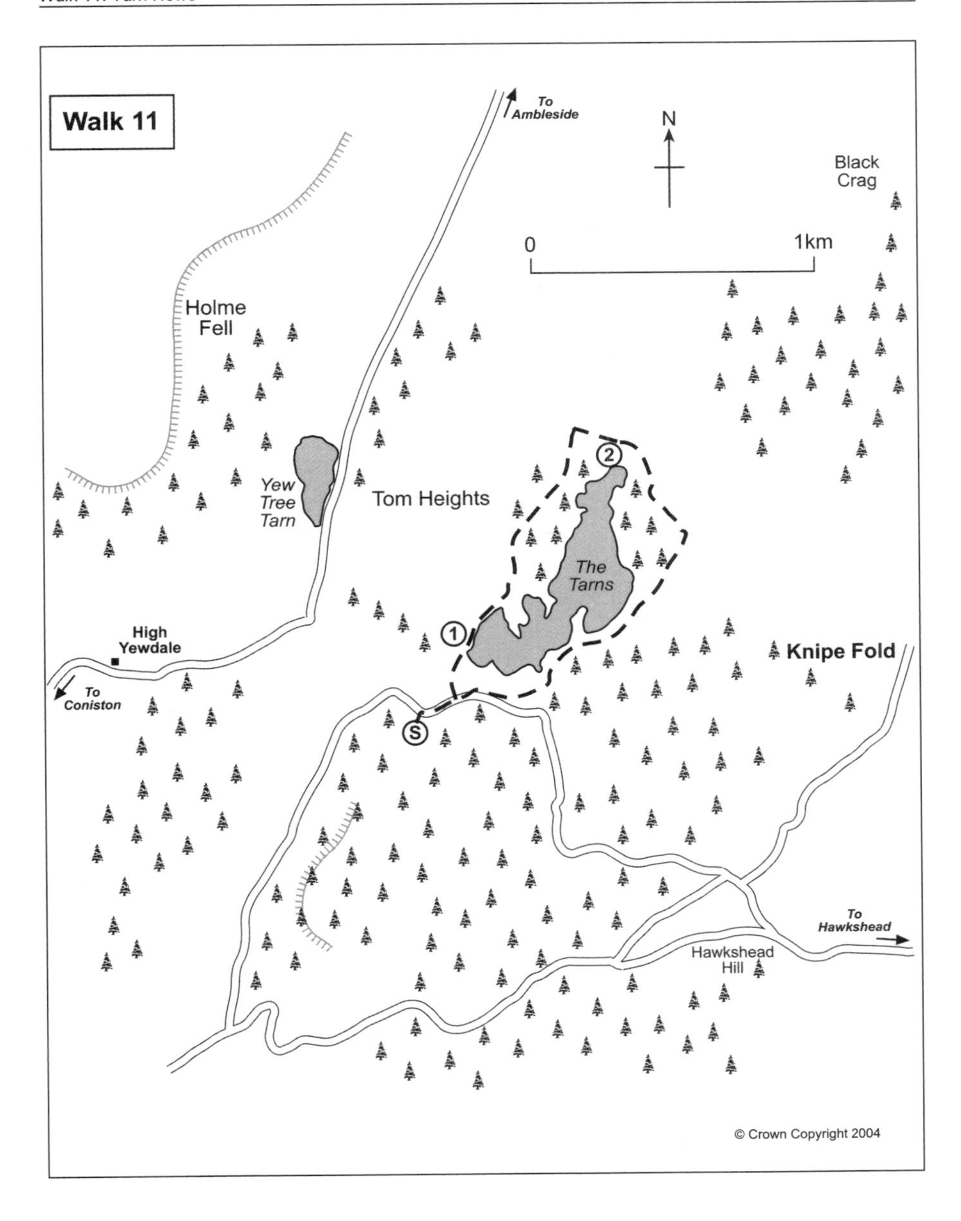
Walk 11
To Ambleside
N
Black Crag
0
1km
Holme Fell
Yew Tree Tarn
Tom Heights
2
The Tarns
1
High Yewdale
To Coniston
S
Knipe Fold
To Hawkshead
Hawkshead Hill
© Crown Copyright 2004

Walk 12: Windermere Shore and Wray Castle

Assessment: Grade 2

The out-and-back section is the easiest possible walk, being level, along a broad firm track. The ascent to Wray Castle is over grass, including a short, steep, slope.

Distance: 5km (3 miles).

Total ascent: 15m (49ft).

Start/car parking: Red Nab car park, accessed from the Ambleside to Hawkshead road, via High Wray, grid reference 385995.

Refreshments: none.

Map: Ordnance Survey Explorer 7, The English Lakes, South Eastern area, 1:25,000.

The Area

The lakeside track is a very pleasant route, allowing appreciation of much of England's largest lake, still attractive despite years of over use. From 2005, the speed limitation should much enhance the quiet enjoyment of the lake by walkers and others. On the far shore are the historic Calgarth Park, White Cross Bay, home of a factory building Sunderland flying boats in World War II, The National Park Visitor Centre at Brockhole, the Langdale Chase Hotel and the Low Wood Hotel. Wansfell Pike, above Ambleside, is very prominent.

Wray Castle is a Victorian sham built by an eccentric, used for many years as a training centre for marine communications.

The Walk

Leave the car park along the broad lakeside track to the north, through woodland which is part of the National Trust Claife Estate,

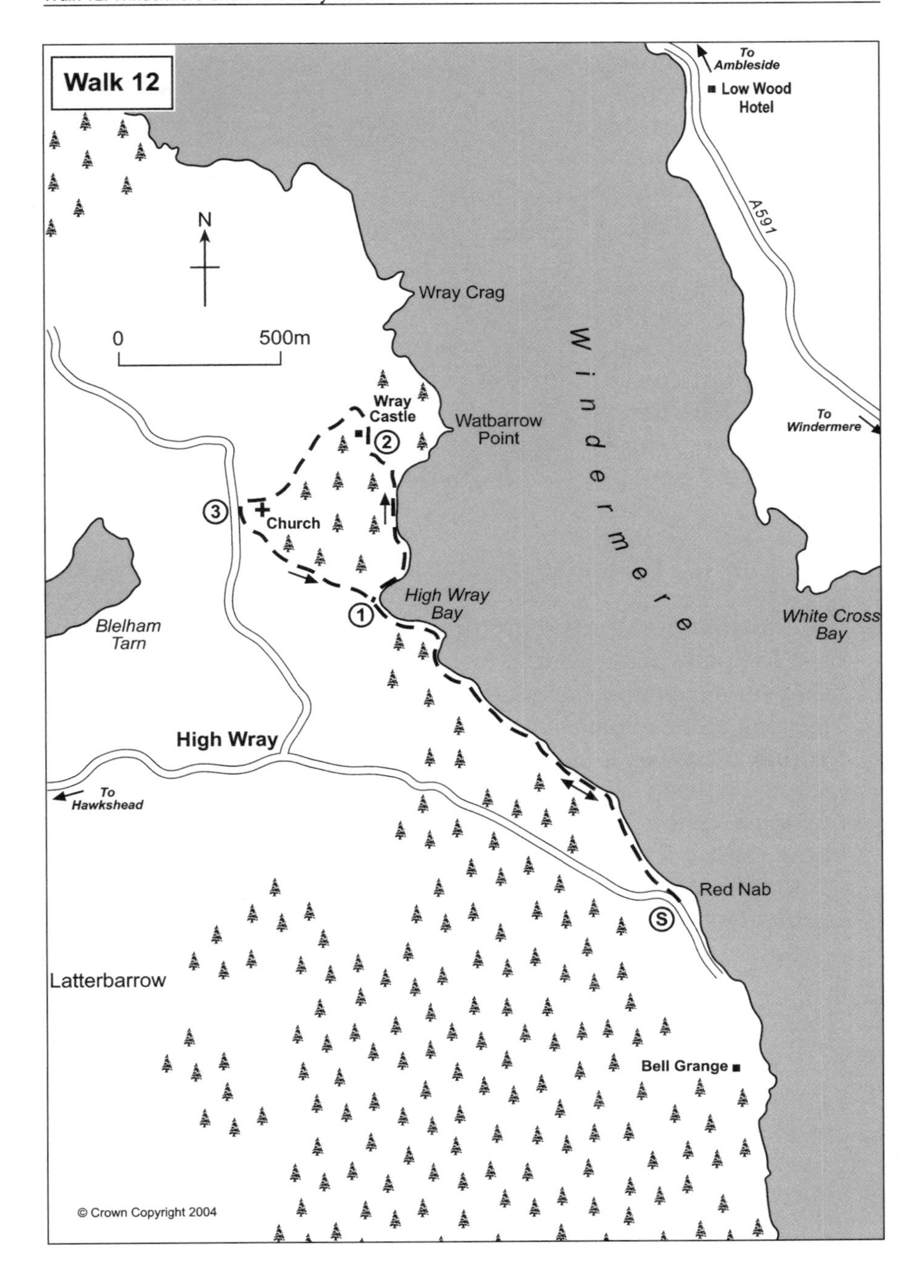
Walk 12
To Ambleside
Low Wood Hotel
A591
N
0
500m
Wray Crag
Windermere
Wray Castle
Watbarrow Point
To Windermere
Church
High Wray Bay
White Cross Bay
Blelham Tarn
High Wray
To Hawkshead
Red Nab
Latterbarrow
Bell Grange
© Crown Copyright 2004

passing a vehicular barrier. The views across the lake include much of the celebrated 'Fairfield Horseshoe' of mountains. Pass a boathouse and cross a stream on a plank bridge before reaching High Wray Bay, with another boathouse. Leave the Claife Estate through a gate, signposted 'public bridleway Wray Church'. Go through another gate, the track now rising gently.

High Wray Church

1. In a further 40m turn right, through a gate, signposted 'permitted footpath Wray Castle. National Trust Wray Castle Estate'. Continue over short grass, a fine area for lakeside picnics, soon passing a third boathouse before reaching the wooded knoll on which Wray Castle stands. Bear left to ascend a steep little grass slope between the trees. Bear left 70m **before** the gate/stile which is visible to the right. Ahead, another stile is soon in view; bear right a few metres **before** the stile, following an evident path to a gate giving access to a roadway by the castle. Follow the vehicular 'way out' sign along the castle terrace, a fine viewpoint.

2. Continue along the castle access road, passing the Dower House before reaching the public road by the gatehouse.

3. Turn left at the road then left again along a signposted bridleway in a few metres. St Margaret's Church, High Wray is to the left. A good track descends with a stream on the right to rejoin the outward route by the gate at point 1. Bear right to return along the lakeside to the car park.

Walk 13: Troutbeck and Brockhole

Assessment: Grade 5

Not a long walk, but a fair amount of uphill pushing, some quite steep. Although the majority of the route is on good surfaces, there are also sections of very rough stone. There are no stiles, kissing gates or other obstructions.

Distance: 4km (2½ miles), not including any distance within the grounds at Brockhole.

Total ascent: 150m (492ft).

Start/car parking: Roadside area for a few vehicles 300m south of Town End, the National Trust property, grid reference 406020.

Refreshments: Café at Brockhole (seasonal).

Map: Ordnance Survey Explorer 7, The English Lakes, South Eastern area, 1:25,000.

The Area

The walk traverses the comparatively gentle farming countryside between Troutbeck village and the shore of Windermere, with good views over the latter.

The well-known Lake District Visitor Centre at Brockhole has a range of indoor exhibitions (open, with the café, during the normal holiday season). Open all the year are the gardens and extensive grounds between the house and the lake shore. Not least among the attractions is a well-equipped children's play area. The only charge at Brockhole is for car parking.

The Walk

Turn left along the road towards Ambleside, rising gently. As the road bends to the right in 100m, go ahead along a walled lane with a 'public bridleway' signpost, starting the long descent, The lake is soon in view. The surface becomes very rough and stony. Pass a derelict barn and then a bank barn. To the left, Orrest Head, above Windermere village, is in view. The surface improves as Middlerigg Tarn is passed, although one section is usually wet and muddy.

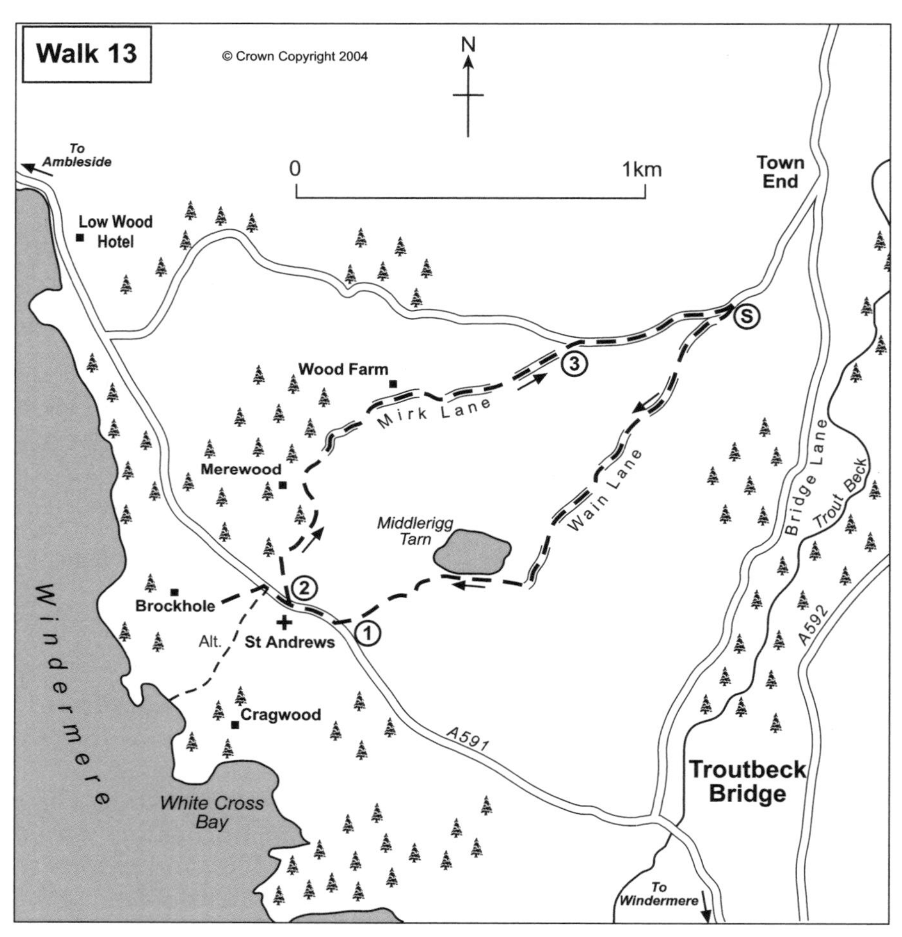

Cross a fast-flowing beck on a tiny bridge, pass a barn and reach the A591 main road.

1. Cross with care, then turn right, along the generous footpath/cycleway. Pass St Andrew's, Ecclerigg, now spick and span after many years of being virtually invisible under rampant undergrowth.

   A left turn along the access drive of Cragwood Country House Hotel ('public footpath' signpost) provides a good, easy diversion directly to the lake shore, with a stile into the Brockhole children's play area.

Farm on Holbeck Lane

For Brockhole, turn left into the car park and follow the signs. Leaving Brockhole, turn right, along the side of the main road for 40m. Cross the road by the central reservation.

2. Turn left along a surfaced road way, signposted 'public bridleway, Mirk Lane'. Pass Merewood Lodge then Merewood Cottages. At once the track becomes comparatively narrow and rough, rising steeply for some distance. After a short descent, bear right before rising again. Go straight on as a footpath joins from the left, downhill to a gate, crossing a stream on a slab bridge and passing a waymark on a post.

Pass Wood Farm, turning left at the surfaced access drive but soon rising steeply on a rough surface, past a waymark on a fence post, to a gate. Continue uphill. Go straight ahead at a junction, with a wall on the right, reaching a gate in 50m. Continue along a walled lane, slightly downhill but soon rising again to a small farm and a junction with a public road (Holbeck Lane).

3. Turn right to walk by the roadside for about 400m to rejoin the outward route and return to the parking area.

Walk 14: Troutbeck and Skelghyll

Assessment: Grade 3

A considerable ascent on a rough stony-surfaced lane at the outset of the circuit. Thereafter, a pleasant easy route with only one short section of narrow path and no significant obstructions.

Distance: 4km (2½ miles). With extension 6km (3¾ miles).

Total ascent: 90m (295ft). With extension 140m (459ft).

Start/car parking: Space for a few vehicles by the side of the Ambleside road, 300m to the south of Town End, at the southern end of Troutbeck village, grid reference 406020.

Refreshments: Take a picnic.

Map: Ordnance Survey Explorer 7, The English Lakes, South Eastern area, 1:25,000.

The Area

The route traverses the gentle hillside above Windermere, essentially hill farming countryside, with fine views over the lake to Claife Heights and the more distant mountains. The old scattered village of Troutbeck (see walk 15) is close at hand, with Town End, owned by the National Trust, as a popular visitor attraction.

The Walk

Cross the road to a lane opposite, signposted 'public bridleway'. The lane, between stone walls, has a rough stony surface, rising steadily to a gate and then a junction with Robin Lane at the top, where there is a well-placed seat.

1. Turn left to continue along Robin Lane, now more level and with a better surface.

   Over the wall to the right is a stone cairn on a knoll, which can be accessed over a stile (not by an ATP!).

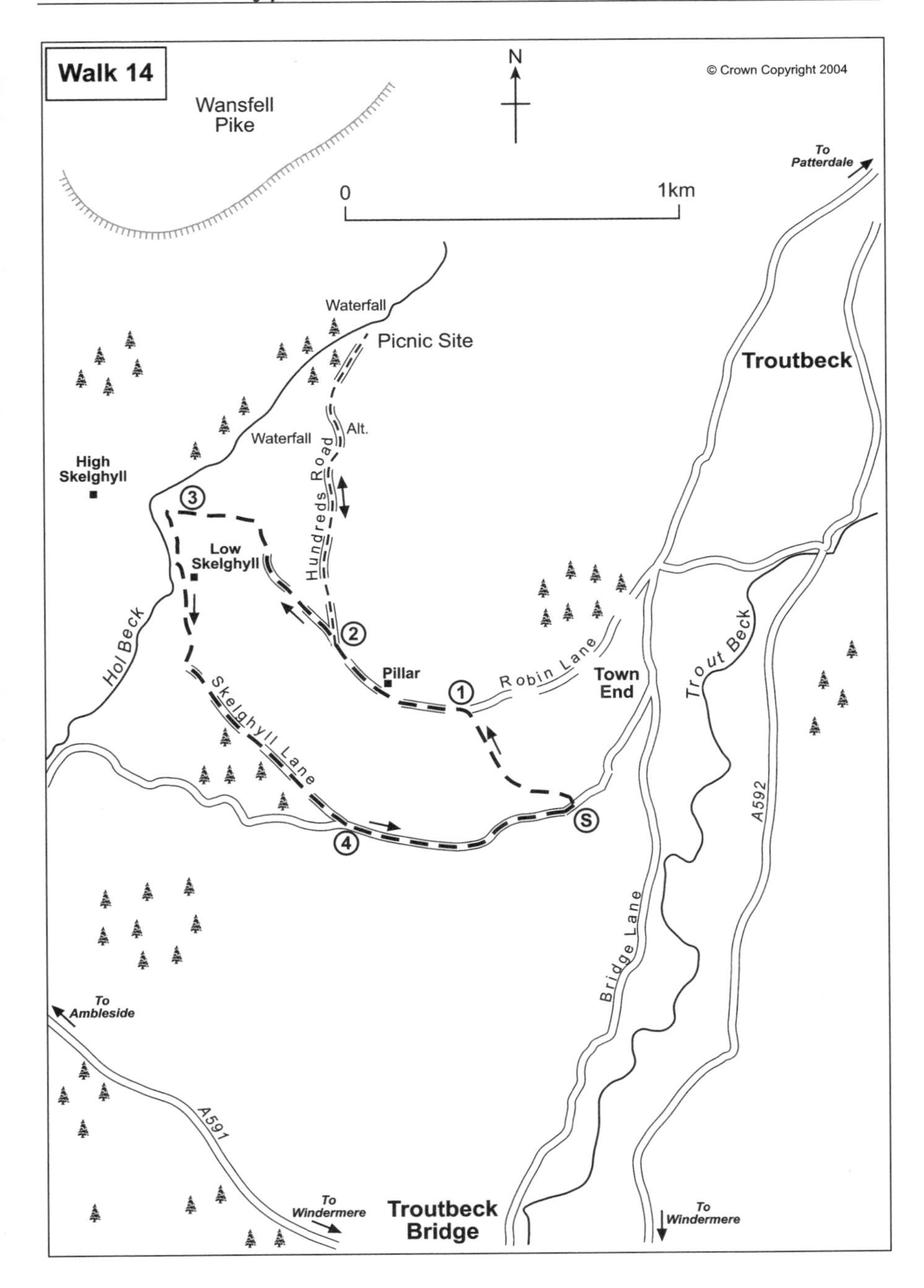

Walk 14
© Crown Copyright 2004
Wansfell Pike
N
0
1km
To Patterdale
Waterfall
Picnic Site
Troutbeck
Alt.
Waterfall
Hundreds Road
High Skelghyll
3
Low Skelghyll
2
Hol Beck
Pillar
1
Robin Lane
Town End
Trout Beck
Skelghyll Lane
S
4
A592
Bridge Lane
To Ambleside
A591
To Windermere
Troutbeck Bridge
To Windermere

Continue to a junction.

To the right is 'Hundred Road' which rises steadily towards Wansfell and can be used as an extension to this route, reaching a lovely waterside picnic site at its top end.

2. For the basic circuit bear left through a gate to descend along a narrower but still excellent path. Wansfell Pike is close ahead/right. Go through a gate, cross two small streams, then take care along a narrow path descending to two gates and a junction by a bridge which crosses a major stream, the Hol Beck. Ahead is High Skelghyll Farm.

3. Turn left, through a gate 'footpath, no cycles' along a broad, easy, firm-surfaced roadway, soon passing Low Skelghyll Farm. Continue along the tarmac-surfaced access roadway, passing a barn and then through a gate before rising a little. Pass a detached house and another barn and join the public road, Holbeck Lane.

4. Turn left to walk by the roadside back to the parking place.

Track near Troutbeck

Walk 15: Troutbeck Village

Assessment: Grade 2

A generally easy walk on good surfaces, with just a small percentage that is relatively gentle uphill.

Distance: 4.5km (2¾ miles).

Total ascent: 45m (148ft).

Start/car parking: Roadside area for a few cars about 300m south of Town End on the road to Ambleside, grid reference 406020.

Refreshments: Mortal Man Inn. 'Cups of tea or coffee' at the post office.

Map: Ordnance Survey Explorer 7, The English Lakes, South Eastern area, 1:25,000.

The Area

The outward route is along the road which links the several farming hamlets comprising Troutbeck village. All hamlets are well up the side of the broad valley, at the level where water comes to the surface; several 'wells' are still evident along the line of the walk. Houses, barns and other farm buildings are seen in close proximity along the roadside, many dating from the 17th century, when sheep farming was profitable and money was spent on new and refurbished buildings. A few Victorian infill houses do, on the whole, integrate well into this remarkable array of traditional Lakeland vernacular architecture.

The return loop is along back lanes, passing the well-known Mortal Man Inn before rising to rejoin the road.

The extended 17th-century farmhouse, Town End, was for centuries the home of the Browne family, 'statesmen' (yeomen) farmers. For many years in the care of the National Trust, it is traditionally furnished to provide a most interesting visitor attraction.

An added bonus for this walk is the view across the valley, over Beatrix Potter's Troutbeck Park Farm, to the great ridge of (from the

Town Head farm, Troutbeck

right) Yoke, Ill Bell and Froswick, rising to the main mass of High Street.

The Walk

From the parking area turn right, towards Troutbeck, passing Kilns, a cottage with a 1700 datestone. Reach a road junction, close to Town End. Opposite is a fine example of a bank barn, still in agricultural use. The extended canopy over the barn doors, forming a gallery, is an unusual feature. A piece of old cruck framing has been reused as a lintel over the door to the north end extension. A little way further, behind an 'L'-shaped barn, is a large very old house, renovated in recent years.

1. At the next road junction is the village institute and the post office, for many years offering 'cups of tea or coffee'. Opposite is the Spinnery, with a fine example of the traditional Lakeland 'spinning gallery' tucked away round the corner. Continue

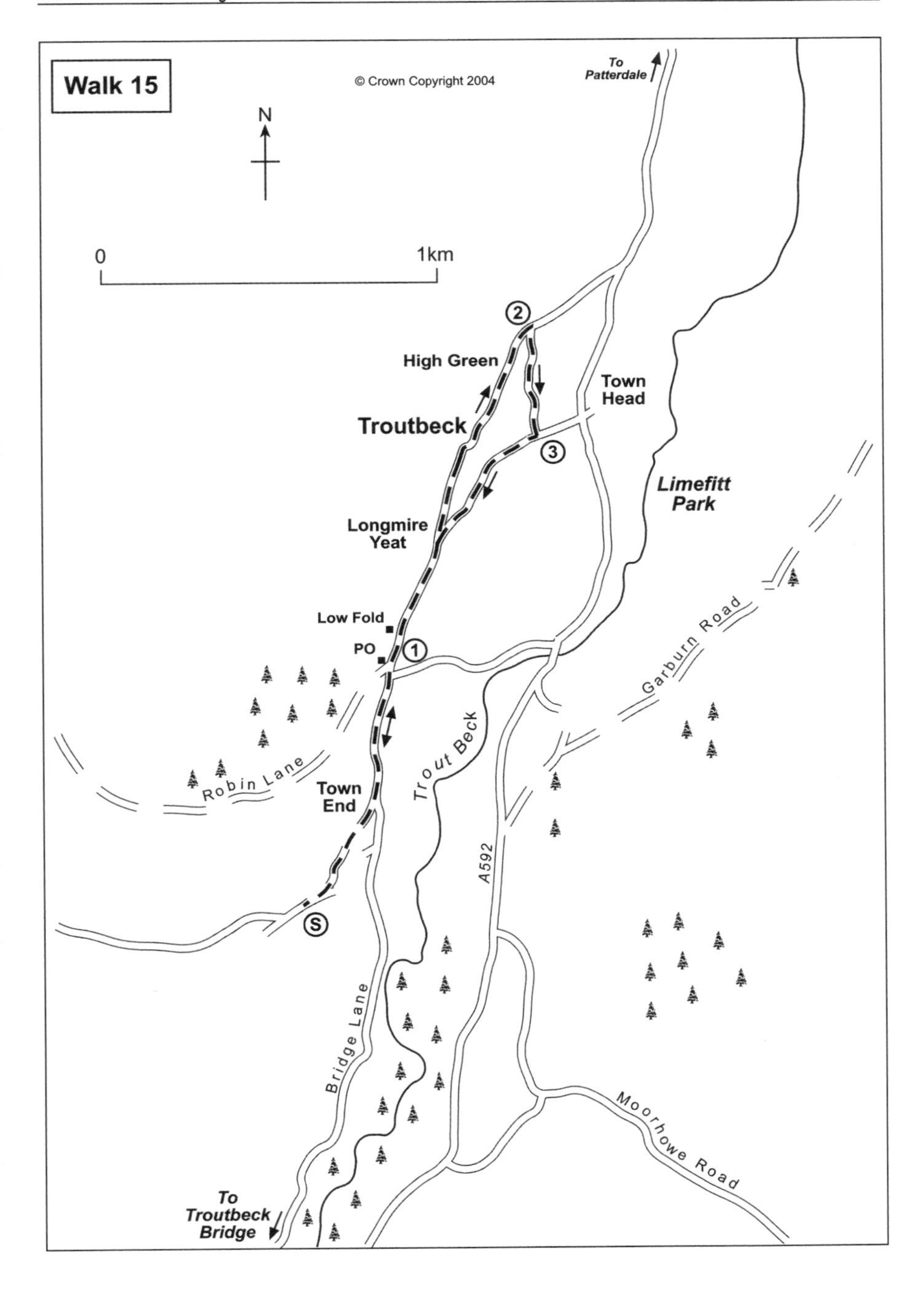
Walk 15
© Crown Copyright 2004
To Patterdale
N
0
1km
High Green
Town Head
Troutbeck
Limefitt Park
Longmire Yeat
Low Fold
PO
Garburn Road
Trout Beck
Robin Lane
Town End
A592
Bridge Lane
Moorhowe Road
To Troutbeck Bridge

along the road, passing the hamlets of Low Fold and High Fold, the latter with its little walled green.

The wells of St John and St James are passed before the next hamlet, Longmire Yeat, is reached. Next is St Margaret's well, with a long barn opposite. The hipped end and the chimney stack are unusual features, as is the Edward VII post box set in the wall at the far end of a Victorian house passed before reaching the Mortal Man Inn, famous for its cautionary sign. The road crosses a stream before an open area by Scot Beck Fold is reached.

2. Turn right here, along a signposted public bridleway. Go right, downhill, at a fork, through High Green hamlet, heading for the Mortal Man Inn. Pass Yew Tree Cottage, with its attractive gallery, turn left at a junction 60m before the Inn, cross a stream and continue along a broad track. (Windermere can just be seen, ahead.)

3. At a four-way signpost in 200m, turn right, along a broad stony track, signposted 'village'. Cross the stream again and rise steadily; some of the track surface is a little rough before the village street is rejoined by Myley Ghyll. Turn left to return to the parking area.

Walk 16: Windermere and Troutbeck

Assessment: Grade 3

For the most part an easy ramble, but the Garburn Road has a rough, stony downhill section. The ascents are at easy gradients.

Distance: 6km (3¾ miles)

Total ascent: 125m (410ft).

Start/car parking: Roadside spaces for a few vehicles close to the junction with the unsurfaced Dubbs Road at the start of the walk at Moor Howe, reached either from the main A591, Kendal to Windermere road (turn north just on the Windermere side of Ings) or from the A592, Windermere to Patterdale (Kirkstone Pass) road (turn east about 1 mile south of Troutbeck church), grid reference 424006.

Refreshments: None en route.

Map: Ordnance Survey Explorer 7, The English Lakes, South Eastern area, 1:25,000.

The Area

Although it uses named roads and tracks to traverse the upland area separating Windermere and Troutbeck, this circuit is comparatively little known. The views, particularly of Troutbeck village, strung along the lower slops of Wansfell Pike, are excellent.

The Walk

Start along the wide, unsurfaced, Dubbs Road, rising gently through the sheep grazing country of Applethwaite Common, passing a small coniferous plantation. Pass the reservoir buildings and then the reservoir itself. The track narrows and the surface becomes rougher, now a lane (droveway?) between stone walls. Go through a gate, continuing to rise, passing another plantation.

Crinkle Crags, Bowfell and the Langdale Pikes

1. In a further 100m, join the Garburn Road (a track connecting Troutbeck with Kentmere). Turn sharp left, downhill.

   The fine views include Troutbeck village and, to the right, Troutbeck Park Farm at the foot of Troutbeck Tongue, owned for many years by Beatrix Potter.

   Descend moderately steeply, a considerable length of the track being over big awkward stones. Bear left at a junction.

2. Bear left at a fork in a further 80m to rise gently along the Longmire Road, another track with a generally good surface but just a little mud.

   The views now include Crinkle Crags, Bow Fell, Great End and the Coniston Fells. Windermere is just visible.

   Go through a gate and along a lane between walls, soon reaching a roadway with tarmac surface.

3. Join the public road, (Moorhowe Road), turning left to return to the parking area. Orrest Head in is view to the right.

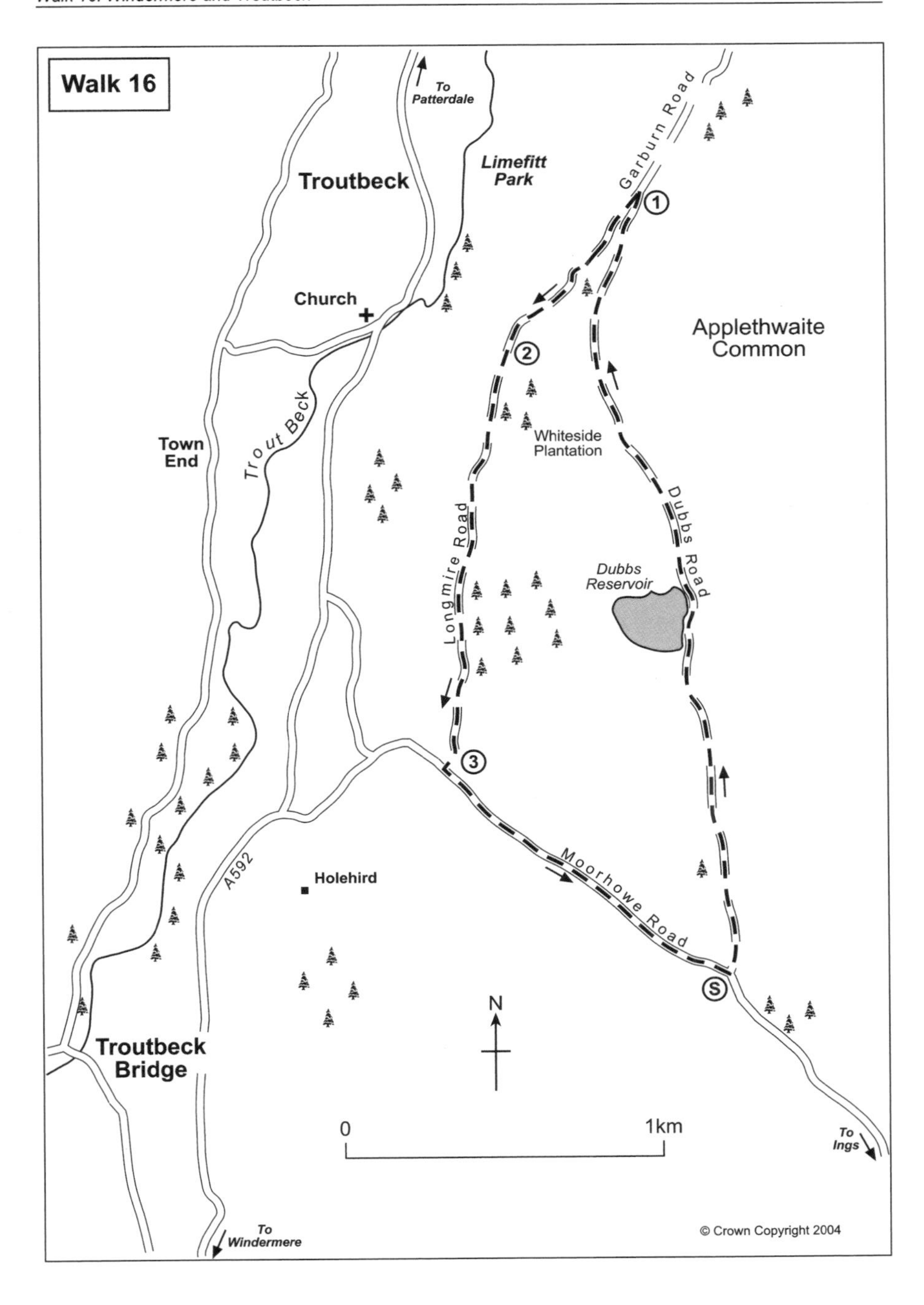
Walk 16
To Patterdale
Troutbeck
Limefitt Park
Garburn Road
Church
Applethwaite Common
Trout Beck
Town End
Whiteside Plantation
Longmire Road
Dubbs Road
Dubbs Reservoir
A592
Holehird
Moorhowe Road
N
0
1km
To Ings
Troutbeck Bridge
To Windermere
© Crown Copyright 2004

Walk 17: Kentmere

Assessment: Grade 3

About 50% of the distance is on tarmac surfaces, the remainder on firm, broad tracks. However, there is nearly 500ft. of ascent, none at steep gradients, and a comparatively long route. Out-and-back from Kentmere hamlet to the reservoir.

Distance: 9.5km (6 miles).

Total ascent: 150m (492ft).

Start/car parking: Limited car parking space by the village institute, grid reference 456041. In high season overflow parking in a nearby field is usually arranged.

Refreshments: none.

Map: Ordnance Survey Explorer 7, The English Lakes, South Eastern area, 1:25,000.

The Area

Kentmere is a very fine valley, largely disregarded for many years as visitors rushed through Staveley on the way to congested central Lakeland. The only road giving access to the valley leaves the A591 at Staveley, winding for 3½ miles to the tiny hamlet of Kentmere itself. A short branch continues to Hallow Bank. Most of the agricultural land, largely created by 19th-century drainage of a lake, is below Kentmere hamlet, above which the valley sides become steeper and rougher, part of the great amphitheatre of Yoke, Ill Bell, Froswick, Mardale Ill Bell and Harter Fell, around the valley head.

The reservoir was created in 1845/6 to regulate supplies of water to the many mills, principally at Staveley and Burneside, which relied on the River Kent for their power. Long disused, it is now an attractive addition to the landscape. Kentmere has the 16th-century church dedicated to St Cuthbert. Close to the hamlet is Kentmere Hall, a farmstead based on a 14th-century defensive pele tower.

Kentmere

The Walk

From the village institute continue along the tarmac-surfaced road, rising fairly gently. At a junction go straight ahead to 'Hartrigg', still rising. The rocky hump ahead is Calfhowe Crag. Pass two cattle grids/gates and then Scales Farm, with bank barn.

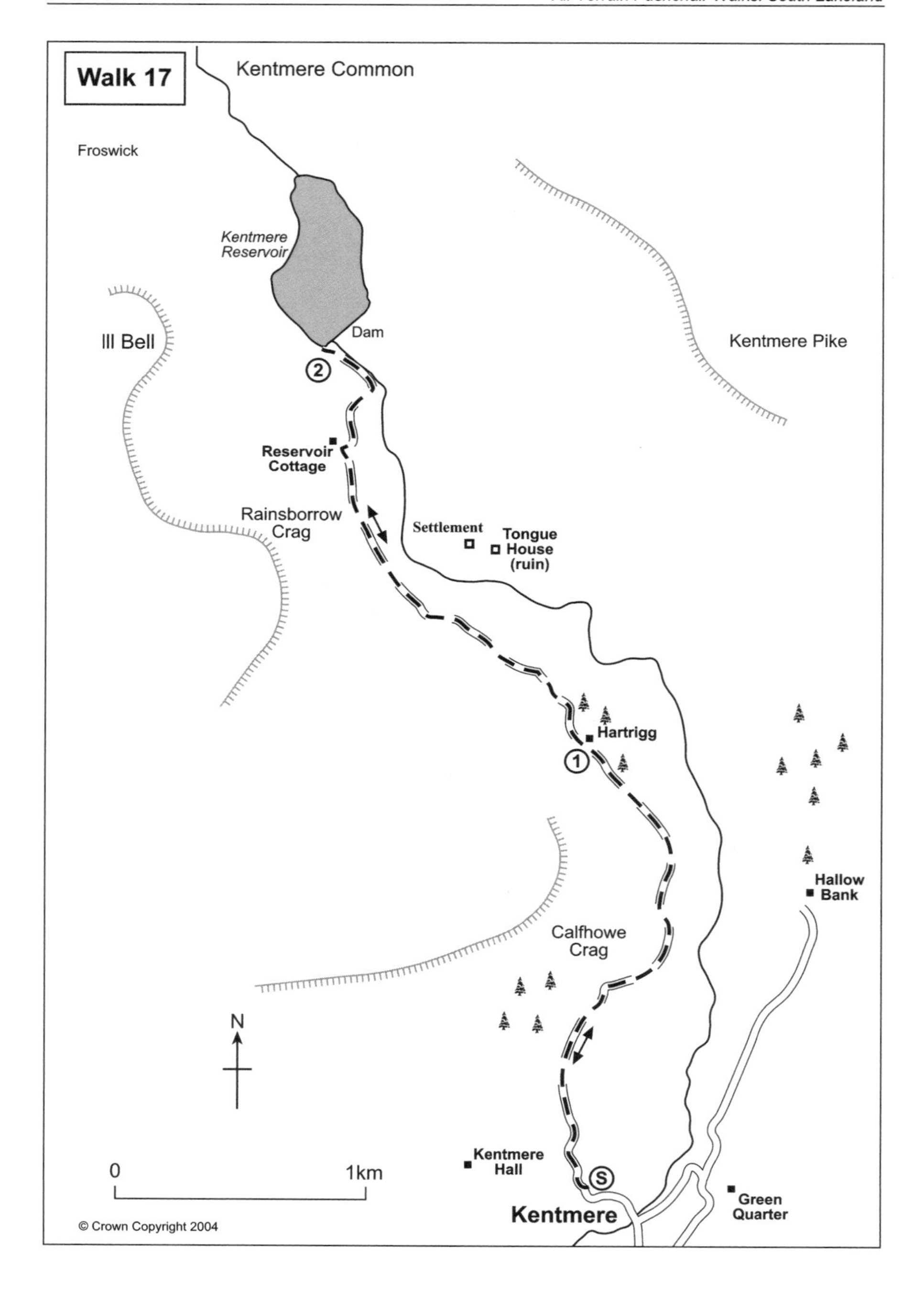
Walk 17
Kentmere Common
Froswick
Kentmere Reservoir
Ill Bell
Dam
Kentmere Pike
2
Reservoir Cottage
Rainsborrow Crag
Settlement
Tongue House (ruin)
Hartrigg
1
Hallow Bank
Calfhowe Crag
N
0
1km
Kentmere Hall
S
Kentmere
Green Quarter
© Crown Copyright 2004

1. Fork left by the entrance to Hartrigg Farm, up to a gate ('public footpath' sign and notice). Go through a gate at the end of the tarmac surface. The track now has some loose stone and a little mud in wet weather as it reaches a wilder landscape, the valley-bottom pastures now being distinctly rough.

   The long high ridge to the right has Kentmere Pike (730m – 2396ft) as its highest point.

   Go through another gate; a rushing stream descends from the left as yet another gate is reached. Rainsborrow Crag is above to the left. Rise towards old quarry spoil heaps, go through a gate, and pass Reservoir Cottage. Continue to rise round a left bend and enjoy the superb view of the valley head.

2. Pass the spillway to rise to the dam, where there are good picnic places. The footbridge below the dam appears to offer an alternative return down the other side of the valley, making a circular route. **Do not be tempted** – the first quarter mile or so is not at all ATP friendly! Return by the same route.

Walk 18: Scout Scar

Assessment: Grade 2

A sharp little ascent is followed by easy walking along the top of a broad ridge **but**, right at the start is a tight kissing gate, necessitating folding or lifting of an ATP.

Distance: Variable – 1.2km (three-quarters of a mile) upwards.

Total ascent: 45m (148ft).

Start/car parking: Free car park close to the summit of the road leading from Kendal to Underbarrow, grid reference 493926.

Refreshments: None en route.

Map: Ordnance Survey Explorer 7, The English Lakes, South Eastern area, 1:25,000.

The Area

Scout Scar is a broad ridge, two miles long, to the south-west of Kendal. It is a surviving part of the rim of the limestone which formerly covered the various other rocks of the Lake District. The west facing side of the ridge is an impressive scarp, whilst the east side slopes gently towards Kendal. Although the summit is no more than 231m (758ft) above sea level, the elevation is sufficient to provide wonderful views of the mountains of the Lake District across the Lyth Valley to the west, Ingleborough and the Howgill Fells to the east and part of Morecambe Bay to the south. Scout Scar is also interesting botanically. Beneath the stunted ash and hawthorn trees is a rich array of lime-loving plants, some growing at the north-western extremity of their British range. In spring, violets and spotted orchids are common.

The 'mushroom' shelter building was erected in 1912 to commemorate the coronation of King George V. In June 2002 it was refurbished to mark the Golden Jubilee of Queen Elizabeth II. Don't miss the internal frieze.

Scout Scar: The 'Mushroom'

The Walk

From the car park, cross the road, turn right for 30m.

1. Turn left, through the tight kissing gate. Rise steeply up the path, a little stony in places, to the top of the ridge. The route is now predominantly on grass, heading south. There are several variations of track on this most popular walking area. For the best Lakeland views keep close to the edge of the scarp on the right (care with young children!). The 'mushroom' building is the only notable feature on Scout Scar itself. Using this as the destination gives a walk of only 1.2km (three-quarters of a mile). For a longer walk, continue beyond the building along the broad, inviting, track

2. A left turn at a large stone cairn, opposite the large farm of Barrowfield, in the Lyth Valley below, at the point where a minor path rises from the valley to join the track, gives a walk of 3.5km (2¼ miles). Reach the crest of the ridge in a short distance then turn left again to return to the 'mushroom' and the car park.

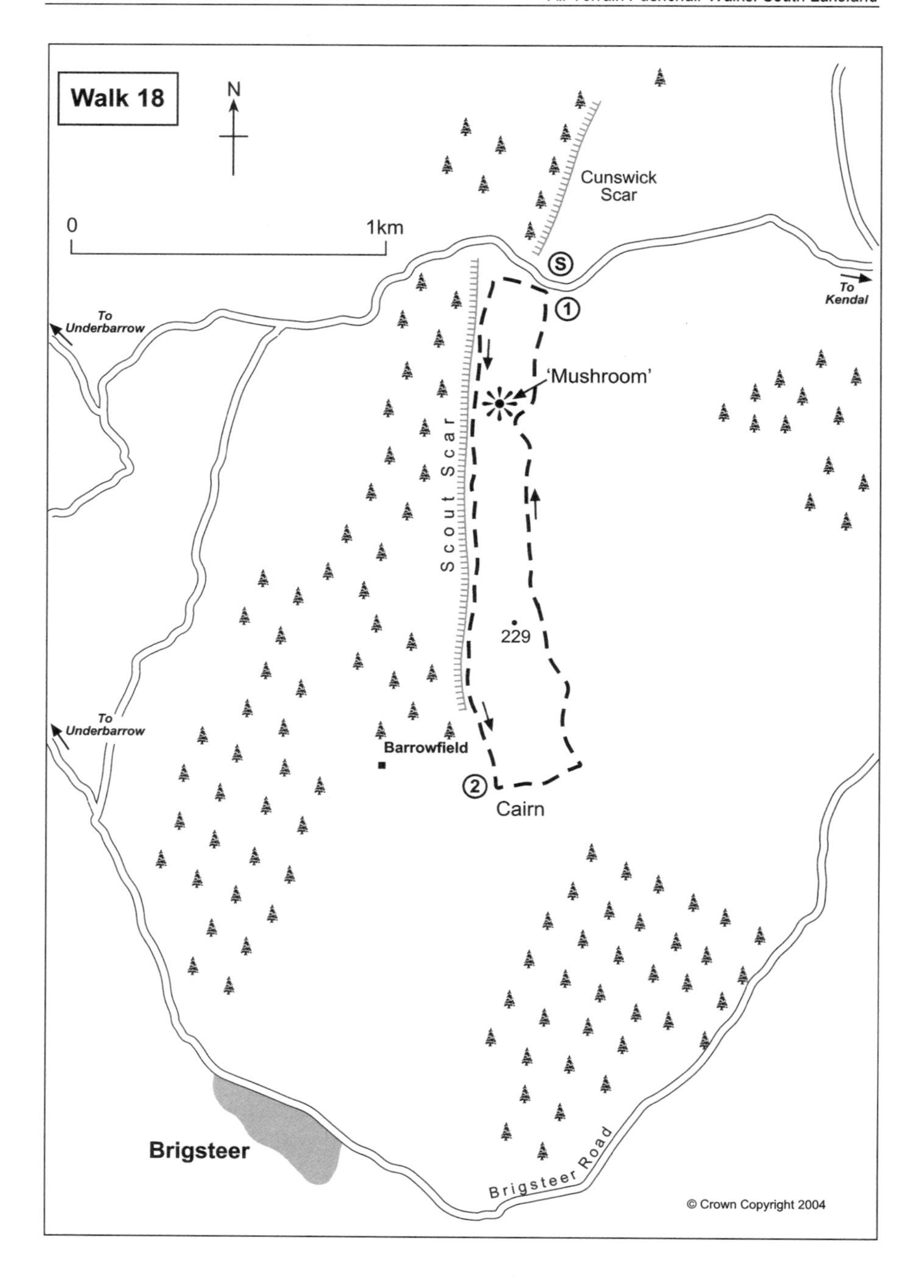
Walk 18
N
0
1km
Cunswick Scar
S
To Kendal
To Underbarrow
1
'Mushroom'
Scout Scar
229
To Underbarrow
Barrowfield
2
Cairn
Brigsteer
Brigsteer Road
© Crown Copyright 2004

Walk 19: Cleabarrow

Assessment: Grade 4

Although this is one of the longer routes, the high grading results almost entirely from the section of path which links the gated tarmac roadway and the wide easy tracks at either end of the walk. This path, a little more than half a mile in length, is in part narrow and awkward, with three difficult kissing gates necessitating the presence of two adults. An easier alternative would be an out-and-back walk to, say, Hag End or Borwick Fold, on tarmac all the way and with very little traffic.

Distance: 6km (3¾ miles).

Total ascent: 110m (361ft).

Start/car parking: Roadside layby on the B5284, Bowness to Kendal road, very close to the clubhouse of the Windermere Golf Club, grid reference 423962.

Refreshments: None en route.

Map: Ordnance Survey Explorer 7, the English Lakes, South Eastern area, 1:25,000.

The Area

The rolling countryside between the A591 and the B5284 roads is quietly attractive, a good example of the 'Silurian' farming landscape of the south-eastern Lakeland fringe. From some of this route there are excellent views of much of the more dramatic Lakeland scenery, before the return via the edge of the Windermere residential area.

The Walk

Start along the roadside towards Crook and Kendal.

The countryside near Cleabarrow

1. In 100m, turn left to follow a minor road with 'gated road ahead' sign. To the left is Cleabarrow Tarn. The road rises fairly gently, passing the edge of an area of light woodland and some outcropping rock. Over a crest, the minor hill visible ahead is Grandsire. Pass the end of the drive leading to Cragg House and descend to Outrun Nook, where a stream flows under the building (a former mill?). Pass the end of the access road leading to Hag End.

2. At a road junction about 300m before Borwick Fold, turn left, uphill, along a road with a grass-grown centre. Pass the drive leading to Yews (on the right) and continue towards Whasdike.

   At a gate there is a magnificent mountain panorama which includes the Crinkle Crags, Bowfell and the Langdale Pikes.

   Close to Whasdike the road turns left, then right

3. At the right turn go ahead to leave the road on a rather vague, signposted, path which crosses rough and often wet ground. The path is marked by occasional waymarks on posts and does improve. Head for School Knott Plantation, descending to cross a little stream and reach the first difficult kissing gate, followed

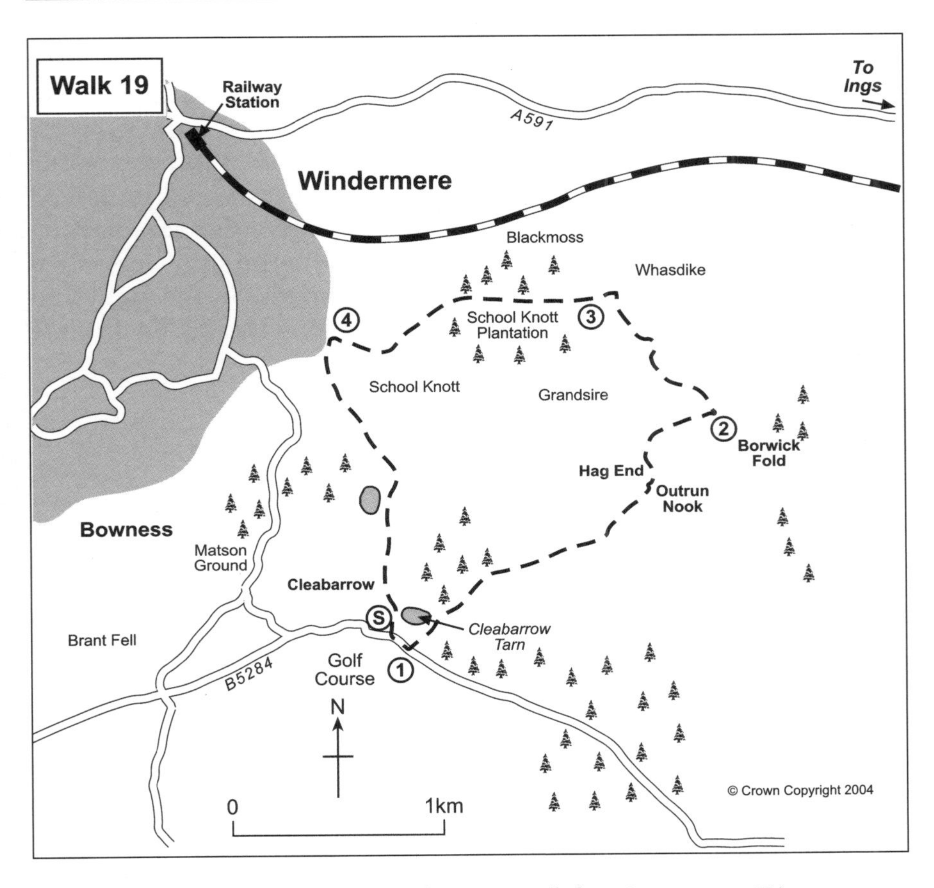

by another stream and the second kissing gate. Rise across moderately rough ground, with the top of School Knott above to the left and fine mountain views ahead. Pass another waymark on a post, with Windermere now just visible. The path across the hillside is narrow, with some exposed rock. Go through a tight kissing gate in the wall on the right before descending fairly steeply on grass paths towards the built-up residential area of Windermere. Where the paths fork, keep generally to the left.

4. Join a broad, surfaced, roadway. Turn left, through a gate. To the right is residential development, to the left is Old Droomer farmhouse, pre-dating almost all other buildings in the area. The road rises after crossing a stream. As the road bends to the right, go ahead through a gate along a broad, unsurfaced track, crossing a stream by a gate. Reach a 'Dalesway' signpost, going straight ahead along a broad track, soon passing an unnamed tarn on the right. Pass through three more gates before reaching the well-spaced houses of Cleabarrow, with the stony lane soon giving way to tarmac. Pass High Cleabarrow on the right and Cleabarrow Tarn on the left before reaching the B5284 and the parking area.

Walk 20: Bowness and Post Knott

Assessment: Grade 3

A fair amount of uphill, some quite steep. Otherwise easy, on good tracks and roadways.

Distance: 2km (1¼ miles).

Total ascent: 90m (295ft).

Start/car parking: Spaces for two or three vehicles by the roadside at a minor junction, grid reference 408969. From the mini roundabout at the foot of Crag Brow in Bowness, drive up the hill for about 100m. Turn right at Helm Road to rise steeply past the Windermere Hydro Hotel. The junction is the fourth on the right, in about 500m.

Refreshments: None en route. Plenty of choice in Bowness.

Map: Ordnance Survey Explorer 7, The English Lakes, South Eastern area, 1:25,000.

The Area

This Bowness-based circuit visits a much-loved viewpoint, Post Knott, with a small diversion to Biskey Howe, also a local favourite. The lakeside holiday settlement of Bowness needs little introduction. Well provided with shops and visitor attractions such as the 'Beatrix Potter Experience' and the Steamboat Museum, it is also a focal point for lake cruising and other water-based activities. Behind the 13th-century St Martin's church is a small area of houses more than 300 years old, the home of the former fishing and boating community. The Hole i' th' Wall Inn is of similar antiquity.

The Walk

Start along the private road leading to Matson Ground, signposted 'permissive path to Post Knott'. In 70m, fork right to a gate with a National Trust 'Post Knott' notice and follow the broad track rising gently through light woodland, with views over Bowness to Claife

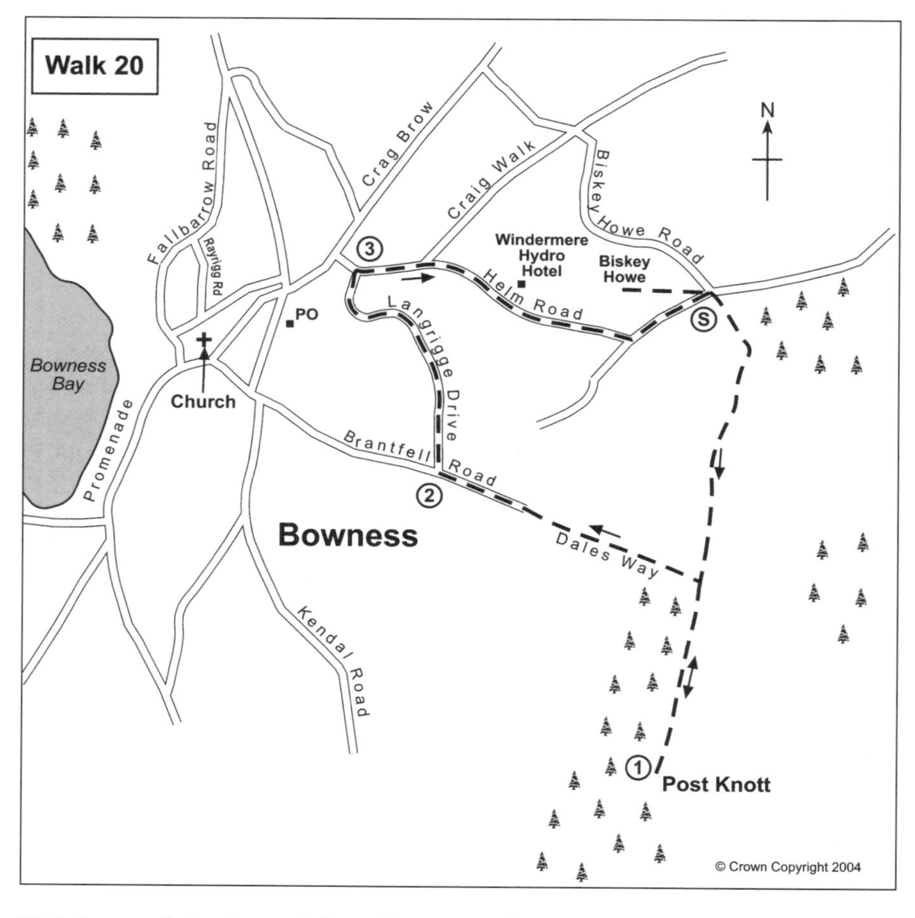

Heights and the Langdale Pikes. Pass the intersection with the Dales Way and continue, the track soon becoming terraced, with occasional wayside seats of some antiquity.

1. At the top go through a kissing gate and up a short grass slope to reach Post Knott, for extensive views along the lake, with Belle Isle, and the Coniston group of fells. There are several seats. Return along the same track, as far as the intersection with the Dales Way. Turn left to descend across a meadow, passing the 'Dalesway Seat', with plaque. At the bottom is a gate and an awkward step. Join the top of Brantfell Road and descend

steeply, now on a tarmac surface. To the right was the site of the former gas works, now the 'Brantfell Walk'.

Biskey Howe

2. Turn right, into Langrigge Drive, a residential avenue connecting Brantfell Road with Helm Road.

3. At the far end of Langrigge Drive, turn right to walk uphill along Helm Road, passing the Windermere Hydro Hotel before reaching the parking area. From this area, a walk of a few metres in the opposite direction to the start of this walk reaches another road junction and the start of a 'wheelchair' path to the Biskey Howe viewpoint, with orientation table, just 50m or so further.

Walk 21: Bowness

Assessment: Grade 1

An entirely easy little walk on firm surfaces throughout.

Distance: 2km (1¼ miles).

Total ascent: negligible.

Start/car parking: Parking area on the cu- de-sac approach road to the Boatman's café, grid reference 401967, or find a roadside space along the Glebe.

Refreshments: Boatman's café, inns, ice cream etc. along the Glebe.

Map: Ordnance Survey Explorer 7, The English Lakes, South Eastern area, 1:25,000.

The Area

A stroll along the Glebe, Bowness's lakeside promenade, followed by a track to National Trust owned Cockshott Point, with the return across fields, passing the former rectory, the pitch and putt course and the cemetery. The whole route is close to the many shops and other visitor attractions of Bowness village.

The Walk

From the Tourist Information Centre at the start of the Glebe, continue along the roadside footpath, with the lake and fine views towards the Fairfield Horseshoe group of mountains on the right, passing several retail and catering premises.

1. As the road bends to the left, go straight ahead, through a gate, along a broad track among the trees, 'leading to Cockshott Point'. The well-surfaced track is broad and easy. As the lake shore is reached there are fine picnic sites and views across to Claife Heights and Belle Isle, including the historic circular house. Continue along the path, heading for the public slipway and many moored boats.

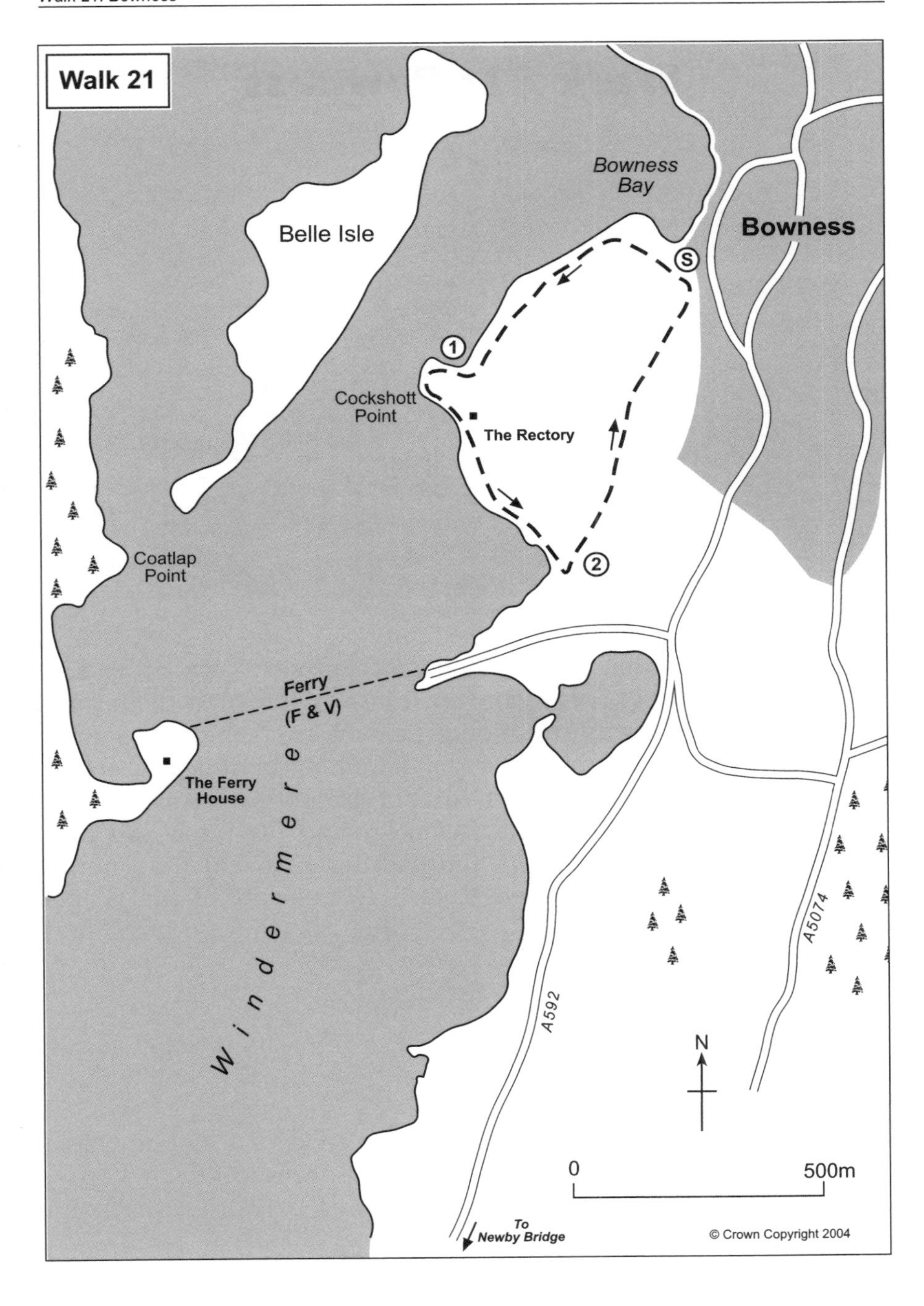
Walk 21
Bowness Bay
Bowness
Belle Isle
Cockshott Point
The Rectory
Coatlap Point
Ferry (F & V)
The Ferry House
Windermere
A592
A5074
N
0
500m
To Newby Bridge
© Crown Copyright 2004

The Glebe, Bowness

2. Go through a kissing gate to join another track. Turn left and go through another kissing gate; the house on the left is the former rectory, with several traditional 'Lake District' chimney stacks. After the track narrows, go through another kissing gate to join the public road. Go almost straight across to continue along Rectory Road, between the cemetery and the pitch and putt course, leading directly to the parking area and the Tourist Information Centre.

Walk 22: Windermere Shore and Far Sawrey

Assessment: Grade 5 (circuit) or Grade 1 (out-and-back).

Although the walk is not long, the combination of steep ascent and rough stony path up the side of Claife Heights puts this route at the limit of ATP walking, needing two adults. The out-and-back route, however, is an extremely easy stroll on level tarmac.

Distance: Circuit, 5km (3 miles). Out-and-back, 3.5km (2¼ miles).

Total ascent: Circuit – 140m (459ft). Out-and-back – negligible.

Start/car parking: Small National Trust pay-and-display car park a short distance along the road from the ferry terminal, grid reference 388955.

Refreshments: Circuit only – Sawrey Hotel, Far Sawrey (with outside seating area).

Map: Ordnance Survey Explorer 7, The English Lakes, South Eastern area, 1:25,000.

The Area

The quieter western shore of Windermere rises quite steeply to Claife Heights, thickly covered by woodland, largely larch, planted about 200 years ago. Despite its popularity, and consequent over-use, Windermere, largest lake in England, is still a most attractive sheet of water, seen at its best out of season, early or late in the day. The outward route of this walk stays close to the shore, with abundant alluring picnic possibilities by the water edge. Views include Belle Isle and many of the smaller islands, Bowness Bay and a great array of boats and water fowl.

Far Sawrey is one of the two small villages, with hotel and shop, along the road from the ferry terminal to Hawkshead.

The Walk

Walk along the roadside towards the ferry terminal. (There is a length of rather narrow track through the woodland which might be preferred.)

Windermere, near Ferry House

1. Turn left at a road junction in 300m to follow the delightful little tarmac road which heads north along the lakeside for almost 1 mile, passing the National Trust Harrowslack car park before reaching a cattle grid/gate and an 'unsuitable for motor vehicles' notice.

2. **This is the end of the out-and-back walk.** Return by the same route.

   For the circuit go through the gate and, in 30m, turn sharp left to commence the prolonged ascent of the side of Claife Heights, with stony and difficult sections of path.

3. Before the hardest section there is a possible 'escape route' by turning left along a track which angles back to the shore road,

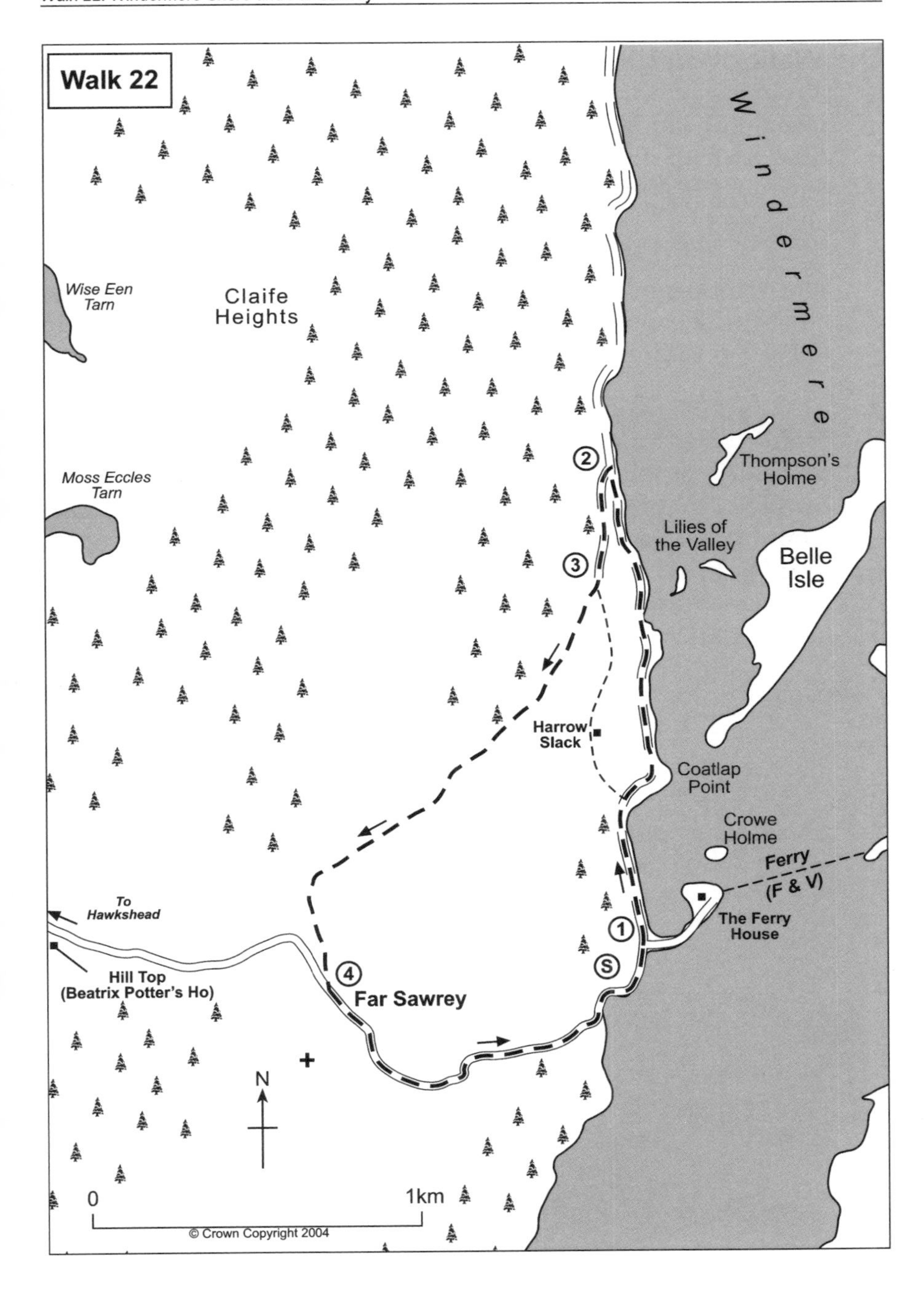
Walk 22
Windermere
Wise Een Tarn
Claife Heights
Moss Eccles Tarn
Thompson's Holme
Lilies of the Valley
Belle Isle
Harrow Slack
Coatlap Point
Crowe Holme
Ferry (F & V)
The Ferry House
To Hawkshead
Hill Top (Beatrix Potter's Ho)
Far Sawrey
N
0
1km
© Crown Copyright 2004

passing behind Harrowslack car park. To continue to the top, go through a gate and along a walled lane At a junction in 50m, go straight ahead following a 'bridleway to Far Sawrey' signpost. After a farm gate, follow the 'public bridleway, Far Sawrey, Near Sawrey, Hill Top' signpost. Go through a waymarked gate.

The long views now include the splendid Coniston group of fells.

The track is now downhill, with a wall on the right, a little rough but quite acceptable. Go through another gate to descend easily to Far Sawrey.

4. At the public road turn left to start the descent towards the ferry. The Sawrey Hotel is to the right. In less than half mile, take the roadside footpath on the right – 'permissive path to ferry via Ash Landing'. Rejoin the road at a gate by the entrance to the Ash Landing Nature Reserve (open to the public, with information boards). Cross the road and go through the gate to continue the descent towards the ferry along a path which leads directly into the car park.

Walk 23: High Dam

Assessment: Grade 3

A long uphill push, on generally good tracks, is required for the outward half of this basically out-and-back walk. To introduce a partially circular element means using a more difficult stony track and crossing a stream on the return.

Distance: 3.7km (2¼ miles).

Total ascent: 95m (312ft).

Start/car parking: Woodland car park accessed either via Finsthwaite village or by heading past Lakeside, then turning left at the Stott Park bobbin mill. From Hawkshead and the north, turn right at the bobbin mill. The car park is at the end of a tiny road to the west, grid reference 369882.

Refreshments: None.

Map: Ordnance Survey Explorer 7, The English Lakes, South Eastern area, 1:25,000.

The Area

Although a little off the beaten track, High Dam is a popular destination for a short walk. Despite its artificial origins, it is in all essentials a pretty tarn in a wooded setting, with numerous enticing picnic sites along the shore. The approach route is entirely within attractive woodland.

Close by are the visitor attractions of Lakeside – steamer pier, Lakeside and Haverthwaite Railway, aquarium and ferry across Windermere to Fell Foot, a popular National Trust site. Even closer is the Stott Park bobbin mill which was Lakeland's last commercially operational mill, restored and open to visitors during the season.

The Walk

Walk past the information table and the vehicular barrier and start

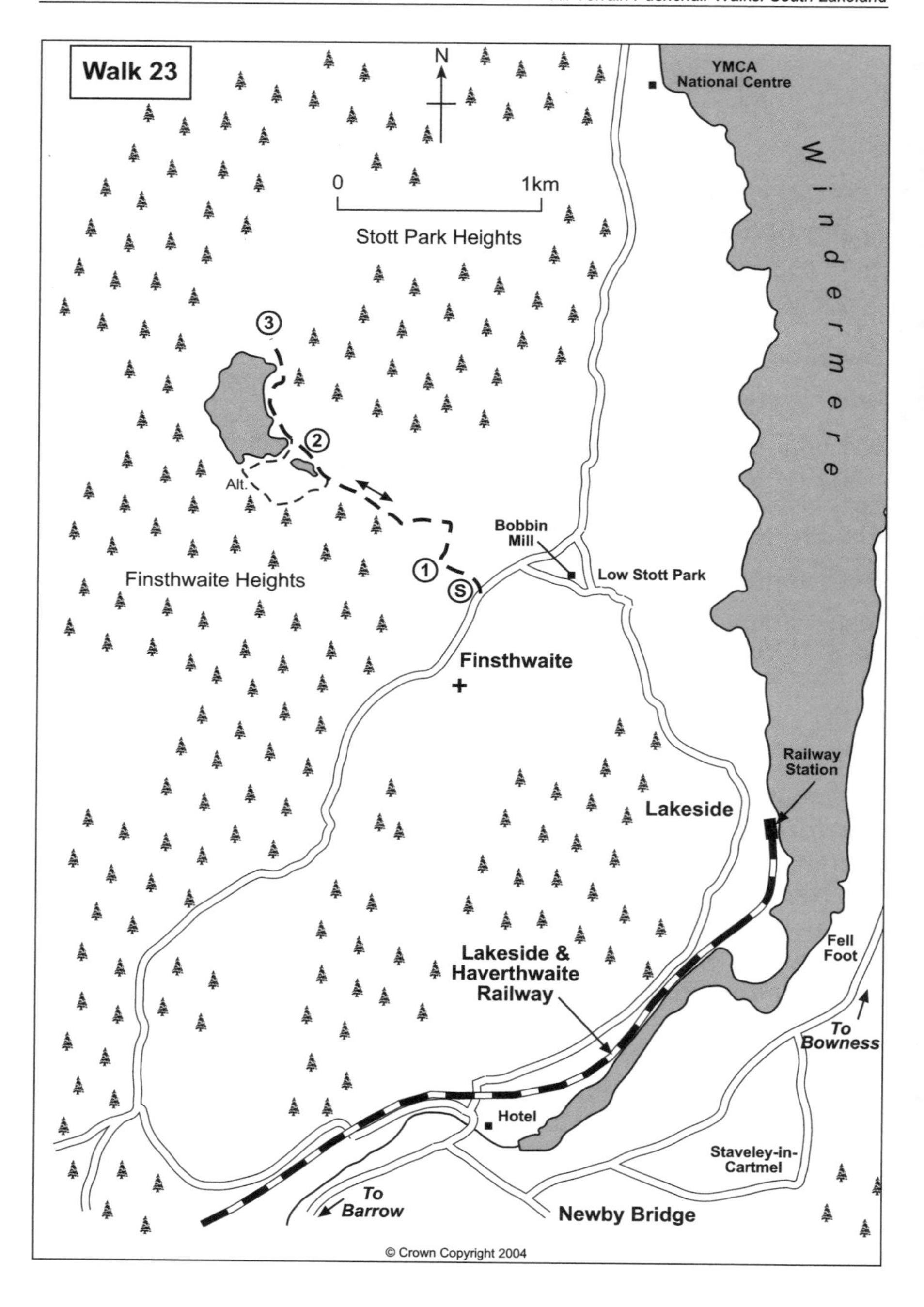
Walk 23
N
0
1km
Stott Park Heights
YMCA
National Centre
Windermere
3
2
Alt.
1
S
Bobbin
Mill
Low Stott Park
Finsthwaite Heights
Finsthwaite
Railway
Station
Lakeside
Fell
Foot
Lakeside &
Haverthwaite
Railway
To
Bowness
Hotel
Staveley-in-
Cartmel
To
Barrow
Newby Bridge
© Crown Copyright 2004

The Bobbin Mill, Stott Park

up the broad rising track, reaching a gate in 50m. Continue, with a rushing stream on the left.

1. In 10m, fork right along a permissive path which winds around the base of a hill, through woodland. Beyond the hill the two tracks rejoin. Bear right to continue uphill to another gate and a fork. Go left here, passing a post with sign in 50m. Go straight ahead, soon reaching a dam and a short section of rough surfaced path. The dam retains a small tarn, 'Low Dam', Cross a substantial footbridge, then another footbridge, to rise again by the rushing waters of the spillway to High Dam, reaching the tarn over another footbridge.

2. **For a short version of the route:** a left turn to take the path along the top of the dam provides a return route, as set out under point **3** (see next page).

   For the full walk: go straight on. A stony section of path soon improves, allowing full enjoyment of the tarn and its surroundings. At the far end the track heads for a kissing gate, whilst to the left a path circumnavigates the tarn. This path has narrow and awkwardly stony sections and is not recommended for ATPs.

3. Return by the same route to the end of the dam (point 2). Either return to the car park by the outward route or cross the top of the dam and continue for a further 150m or so. Turn left to follow an obvious track through the trees, wet in places. Pass a waymark on a post and cross a stream. Stay with the main track at a fork (white waymark on post), descending to cross the outfall stream from the dam. Rejoin the outward route in a few metres, turning right to return to the car park.

Walk 24: Grizedale Forest

Assessment: Grade 4 (circuit) or Grade 1 (out-and-back)

The circuit is mainly along wide, firm-surfaced, forest roadways, without gates or stiles, but there is a prolonged uphill section after Bogle Crag car park and a short, steep downhill on a rough path towards the end of the circuit. The short out-and-back walk poses no difficulty whatsoever.

Distance: (full circuit) 4.5km (2¾ miles). Short out-and-back walk, 2km (1¼ miles).

Total ascent: 110m (361ft).

Start/car parking: Spacious pay-and-display car park with picnic tables at the former Grizedale Hall, close to the main part of the Visitor Centre, grid reference337943. Approached from Hawkshead along the minor road to the south, turning right in less than half mile, via Roger Ground.

Refreshments: Café at Grizedale Visitor Centre.

Map: Ordnance Survey Explorer 7, The English Lakes, South Eastern area, 1:25,000.

The Area

Grizedale (the valley of the pigs) is extensively covered by woodland owned and managed by Forest Enterprises, with a comprehensive visitor centre. The recommended car park is on the site of the former Grizedale Hall, a prisoner of war camp during World War II. Although the forestry is commercial, much attention is paid to conservation and to environmental considerations generally. A notable feature of the forest is the large number of wood sculptures, delightful for children, mainly placed along the numerous trails which wind through the woodland.

The Walk

Leave the car park by the tarmac track at the far end; there are multiple signposts including 'Ridding Wood Trail', soon reaching the first sculpture. Go to the right at a post with blue, white and green markings, by a curious circular wall, continuing past wooden xylophones along a track a little way up the valley side.

Wooden 'xylophone', Grizedale Forest

To the right, below, look out for the animals on the roof of an old building.

Pass a shelter, then a marker post, ignoring the footbridge to the right, to reach a child-sized shelter and marker post.

1. Turn sharp right beside the stream, cross the stream on a little bridge and go straight ahead at a fork, the path now narrow but adequate.

2. Reach an open area with a mosaic circle of forest creatures. **This is the end of the short walk** and from here, you return initially by the same route; a variation can be made by forking right in a short distance before bearing left to cross the stream on the high footbridge.

3. **For the full walk:** from the circle, go straight ahead, down a short but steep narrow path descending to the public road. Turn left, towards Satterthwaite.

4. In about 500m, turn left at Bogle Crag car park (with picnic area), signposted 'Bogle Crag trail'. Pass a vehicular barrier to rise steadily along a firm surfaced roadway through mixed wood-

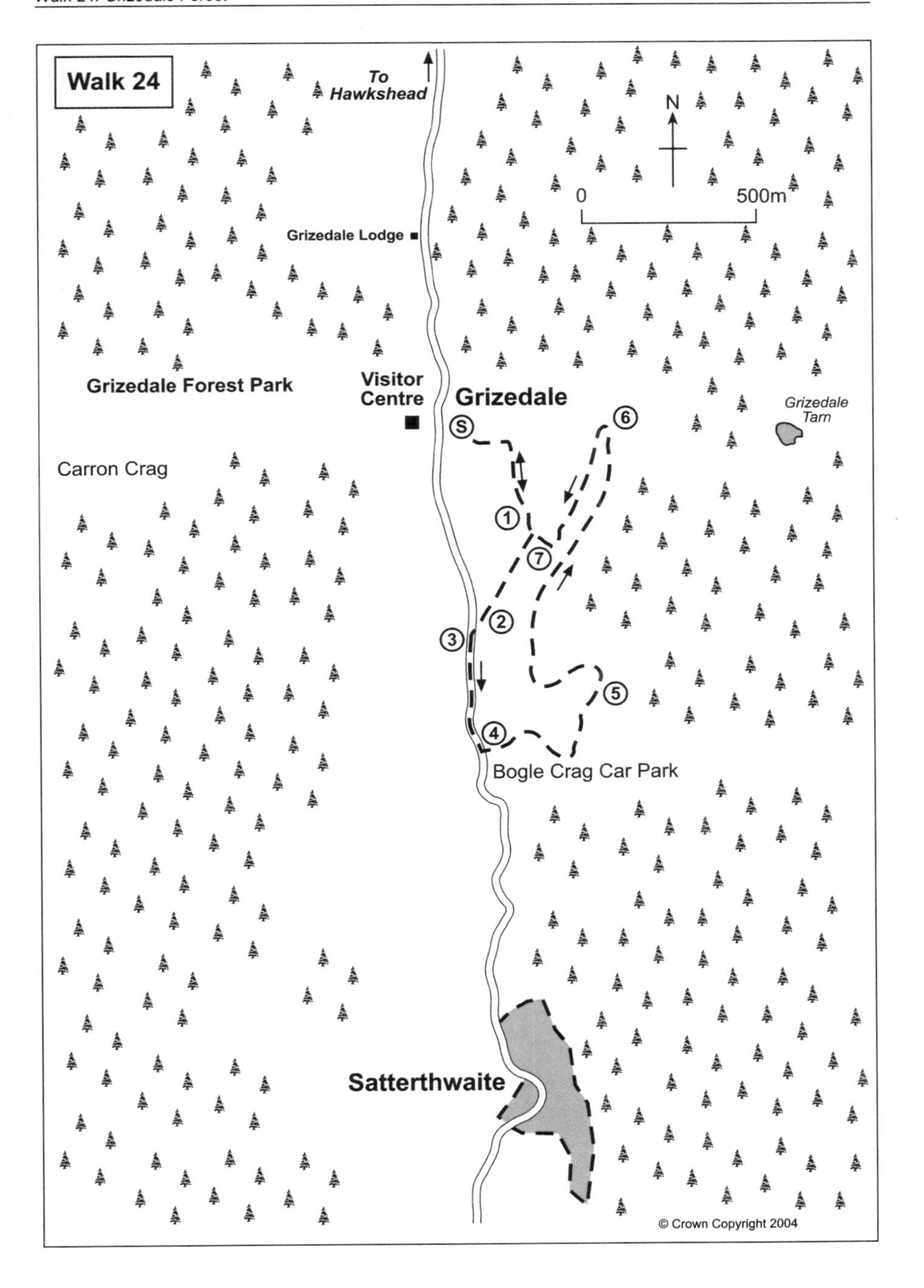
Walk 24
To Hawkshead
N
0
500m
Grizedale Lodge
Grizedale Forest Park
Visitor Centre
Grizedale
Grizedale Tarn
Carron Crag
S
1
2
3
4
5
6
7
Bogle Crag Car Park
Satterthwaite
© Crown Copyright 2004

land. To the left is a purple marked post and a stream. Bear right, then left, passing another purple marker, still rising. Ignore a path to the right; there are now cycle route waymarks.

5. At a major junction go straight ahead, slightly downhill, soon bearing strongly to the left, passing a prominent rock face and a white marker post.

Through the trees there are views to the highest part of the forest, Carron Crag (314m – 1031ft).

Continue along a long level section, passing another white post. Pass the foot of a flight of steps.

6. In a further 30m, turn left at a yellow waymark to descend steeply for 30m along a stony track to a 'T' junction. Turn left (white and green marker post) to descend gently along the valley side on an adequate path, with a stream below to the right, as far as another 'T' junction.

7. Turn right to follow the green and white posts on a steeply descending path with stones and tree roots underfoot, for 100m. At the junction at the bottom turn right, along a well made broad track, with blue, green and white marker. Go left to cross the high footbridge over the stream and rejoin the outward route back to the car park.

Walk 25: Hawkshead and Hawkshead Moor

Assessment: Grade 4 (or, with variation, Grade 3).

This is a comparatively long walk with a good deal of ascent. Although most of the surfaces are good, there are some stony, narrow, sections of footpath. No stiles or difficult gates. Using the minor road as a variation on the return route reduces the required effort.

Distance: 6.5km (4 miles). Variation 5km (3 miles).

Total ascent: 165m (542ft). Variation 135m (443ft).

Start/car parking: Forest Enterprises car park (free) with picnic tables. By the side of the minor road connecting Hawkshead and Grizedale, via Roger Ground, grid reference 344965.

Refreshments: Variety of inns and cafés in Hawkshead.

Map: Ordnance Survey Explorer 7, The English Lakes, South Eastern area, 1:25,000.

The Area

The former market town of Hawkshead is unlike anywhere else in Lakeland, a compact old settlement of charming little squares and alleyways, an immensely attractive and popular centre. Of particular interest are the church, the former grammar school attended by William Wordsworth, the Beatrix Potter Gallery, and Ann Tyson's Cottage. Abundant inns and tea shops cater for the needs of visitors.

Hawkshead Moor is at the northern end of the huge area of Grizedale Forest, owned and managed as commercial woodland by Forest Enterprises. For many years it has been walker (and cyclist) friendly. There is a visitor centre further along the minor road from Hawkshead to Grizedale.

Roger Ground and Walker Ground are place names dating from the time of the dissolution of the monasteries by King Henry VIII in

1539/40. Parcels of the lands formerly owned by the great Furness Abbey were sold off to individuals, whose names have endured over the subsequent centuries.

The Walk

Start by walking past the vehicular barrier at the back of the car park. Go straight ahead at a junction in 25m.

1. At the next (three-way) junction in about 200m, turn right to follow a broad forest roadway, more or less level for a total of 1km (two-thirds of a mile).

2. One hundred metres after a track joins from the left, turn right at a waymarked bridleway. There is a sign 'Permitted bridleway. This route goes to Hawkshead village'. There is a stone wall on the right as the path heads for Hawkshead. Cross a stream, go through a gate and continue by the side of the stream, with excellent views of the mountains beyond Ambleside. The old buildings of Walker Ground are soon reached, with a 'Hawkshead' signpost beyond. Carry on to the village, passing Ann Tyson's Cottage before reaching the centre. Turn right to follow the main street as far as a little green by the public conveniences.

3. Turn right (signpost 'Hawkshead Church and Walker Ground') to walk past the former Grammar School and through the churchyard. Bear left to a gate at the far boundary. There are two more gates, one signposted 'Roger Ground', with a left turn, before that hamlet is reached. Turn right to walk up the steep little public road for 100m. **For the variant route** (easier!), continue along the road back to the car park.

4. For the full circuit turn left ('Howe Farm' signpost). Initially on tarmac, the path soon becomes grassy after passing 'Springfield' and crossing a gated footbridge. Pass a static caravan site, with Esthwaite Water in view ahead. At Howe Farm go left, through 2 gates, to reach the farm access road. Continue to the public road. Turn right to walk by the roadside for almost 400m.

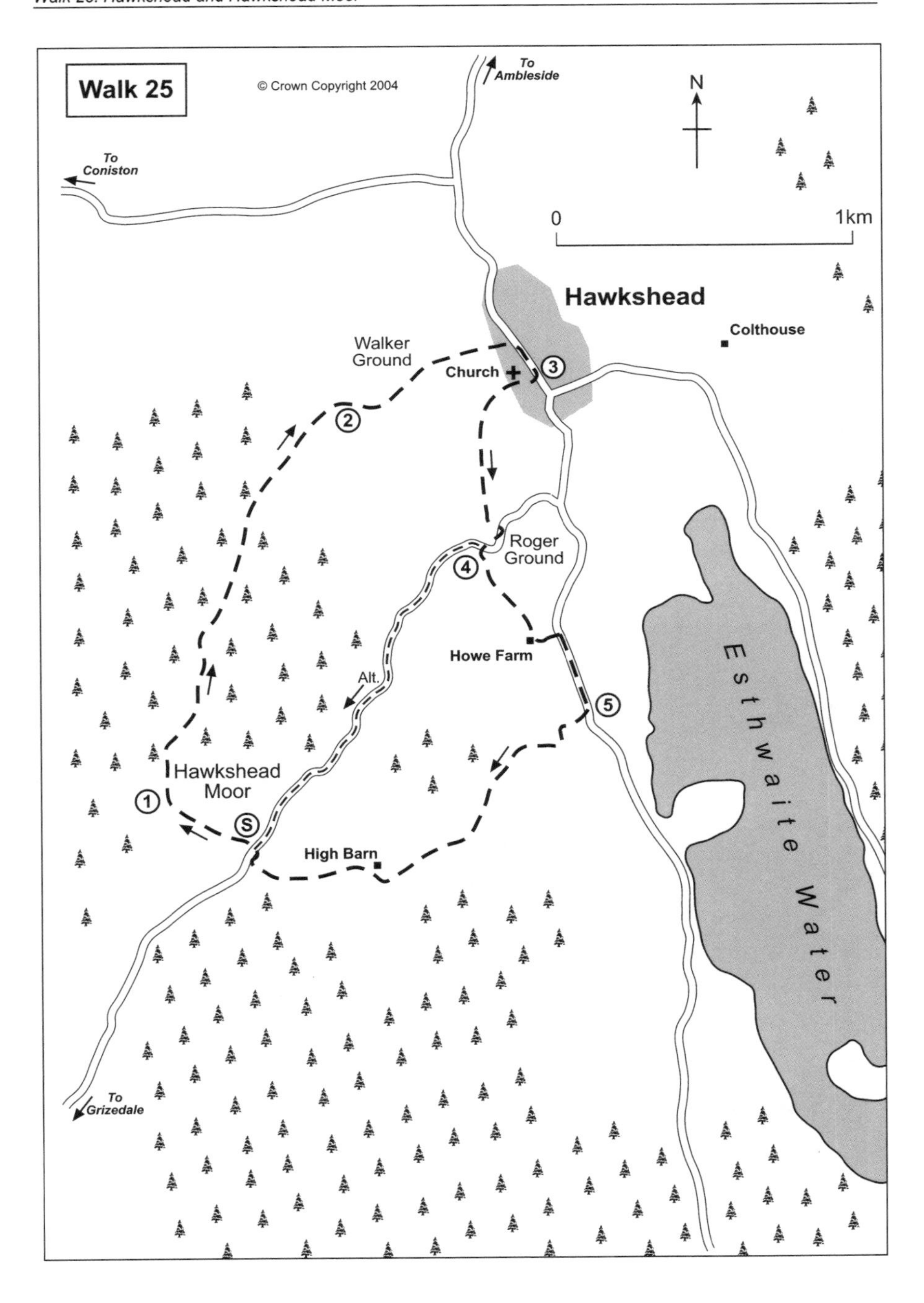

Walk 25
© Crown Copyright 2004
To Ambleside
N
To Coniston
0
1km
Hawkshead
Colthouse
Walker Ground
Church
3
2
Roger Ground
4
Howe Farm
Alt.
5
Esthwaite Water
Hawkshead Moor
1
S
High Barn
To Grizedale

5. Take the second access drive on the right, with a 'public footpath' sign. Pass through a small hamlet with old buildings and through the grounds of the last house, Elder Ghyll, to commence the long ascent back to Hawkshead Moor. Cross a vigorous beck on a footbridge and follow the steep and rather rough and muddy path along the side of a wooded valley. Leave the woodland at a gate, cross a stream on a tight little bridge and follow the waymarks on posts, which mark the line of the path up the open hillside.

As height is gained, the views back to the Fairfield Horseshoe and the mountains above Troutbeck are impressive.

There is some wet ground and several gates before the isolated dwelling 'High Barn' is reached. Pass between the house and its outbuilding, then follow the access drive is it rises steadily to the Hawkshead to Grizedale road, passing a 'Moor Top' signpost en route. At the public road turn right to return to the car park.

The Queen's Head Inn, Hawkshead

Walk 26: Near Sawrey and Moss Eccles Tarn

Assessment: Grade 3

The steady ascent is the only significant factor in assessing this straightforward out-and-back walk. All surfaces are good and there are no stiles or awkward gates.

Distance: 4.5km (2¾ miles).

Total ascent: 100m (328ft).

Start/car parking: National Trust and public car parks in Near Sawrey, grid reference (public) 369957.

Refreshments: Tower Bank Arms, Buckle Yeat Cottage (seasonal).

Map: Ordnance Survey Explorer 7, The English Lakes, South Eastern area, 1:25,000.

The Area

Near Sawrey is Beatrix Potter country. Her home at Hill Top is a very popular visitor attraction in the care of the National Trust and many of the village properties appear in the illustrations in the much loved children's books. For many years she kept a rowing boat on Moss Eccles Tarn. The gentle countryside is unfailingly pleasant and there are wonderful views to the mountains.

The Walk

From either car park walk towards the Tower Bank Arms.

1. Turn left along the 'village street', soon passing a substantial farm on the left, as the road loses its tarmac surface. Continue uphill to a gate, pass a former quarry on the left and a farm building on the right before the track becomes more level.

2. At an important junction of tracks follow 'Bridleway Claife Heights', then pass a waymark on a post, rising gently. Keep right at an apparent fork.

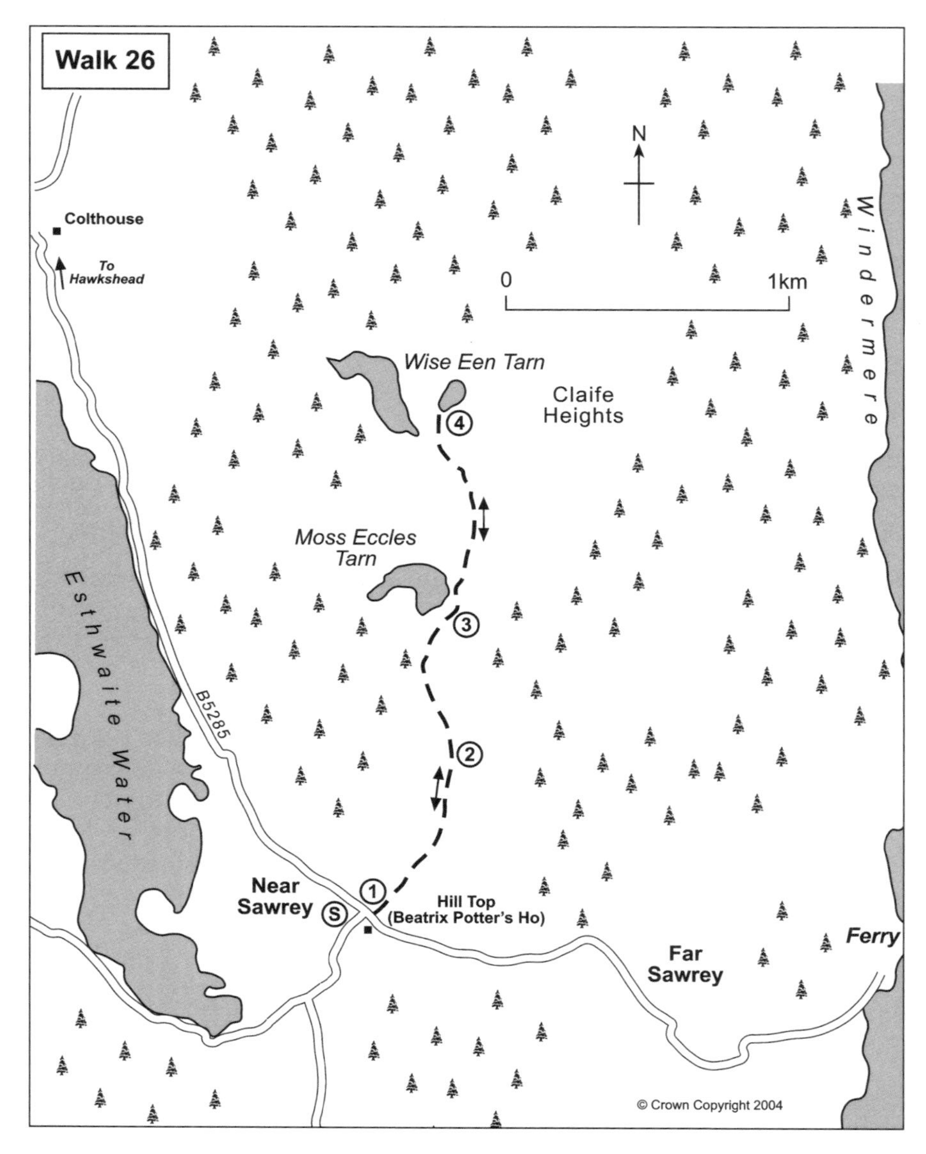

3. Reach Moss Eccles Tarn, with lovely picnic spots and mountain views, particularly of the Coniston group of fells. Continue to rise on a good track, passing a waymark on a post before reach-

Moss Eccles Tarn

ing a waymarked gate (superb viewpoint – including Crinkle Crags, Bowfell and the Langdale Pikes) and then Wise Een Tarn.

4. Return by the same route.

Walk 27: Tilberthwaite and Little Langdale

Assessment: Grade 3

A fair amount of uphill. Apart from a short section near Hodge Close, surfaces are generally good, although there are sections likely to be wet. The extension to the Three Shires Inn necessitates carrying over a footbridge.

Distance: 5.5km (3½ miles). Three possible extensions are suggested below. Each of the first two adds 1.5km (1 mile) to the overall distance. The Hodge Close extension is shorter.

Total ascent: 90m (295ft).

Start/car parking: Car park close to Yewdale Beck, reached by the little Tilberthwaite road which leaves the Ambleside to Coniston road less than two miles north of Coniston village, grid reference 305011.

Refreshments: None en route. Possible extension to the Three Shires Inn (see below).

Map: Ordnance Survey Explorer 7, The English Lakes, South Eastern area, 1:25,000.

The Area

Little Langdale is a delightful valley, more relaxed than its more famous Great neighbour, with the hamlet which includes the Three Shires Inn as the focal point. Slater Bridge is a superb packhorse bridge, combining a stone arch with a primitive clapper which is not ATP-friendly!

The Tilberthwaite area is dominated by the remains of extensive quarrying of which the great water-filled hole near Hodge Close and the 'cathedral' near Slaters Bridge have become visitor attractions.

At Tilberthwaite

The Walk

Turn left out of the car park to walk along the tarmac surfaced roadway. Go through gates to pass High Tilberthwaite Farm, leaving the farm and the tarmac through another wide gate. Continue along the broad track, gently uphill to a gate, pass old quarry spoil heaps, softened by silver birch trees.

1. Bear right at a fork (the track to the left has a locked gate), downhill, passing below Moss Rigg Wood and Brooklands Bungalow, soon reaching Little Langdale Beck at a ford and footbridge.

2. **For the diversion to Slater Bridge** and the 'cathedral' turn left here to follow a good track for about 400m. The bridge is to the right; the great roofed-over quarry hole is up an awkward little path to the left.

   For the diversion to the Three Shires Inn, cross the bridge and take the little lane on the far side up to the Little Langdale road. The Three Shires Inn is to the right.

   To continue the basic circuit, retrace a few metres to a major

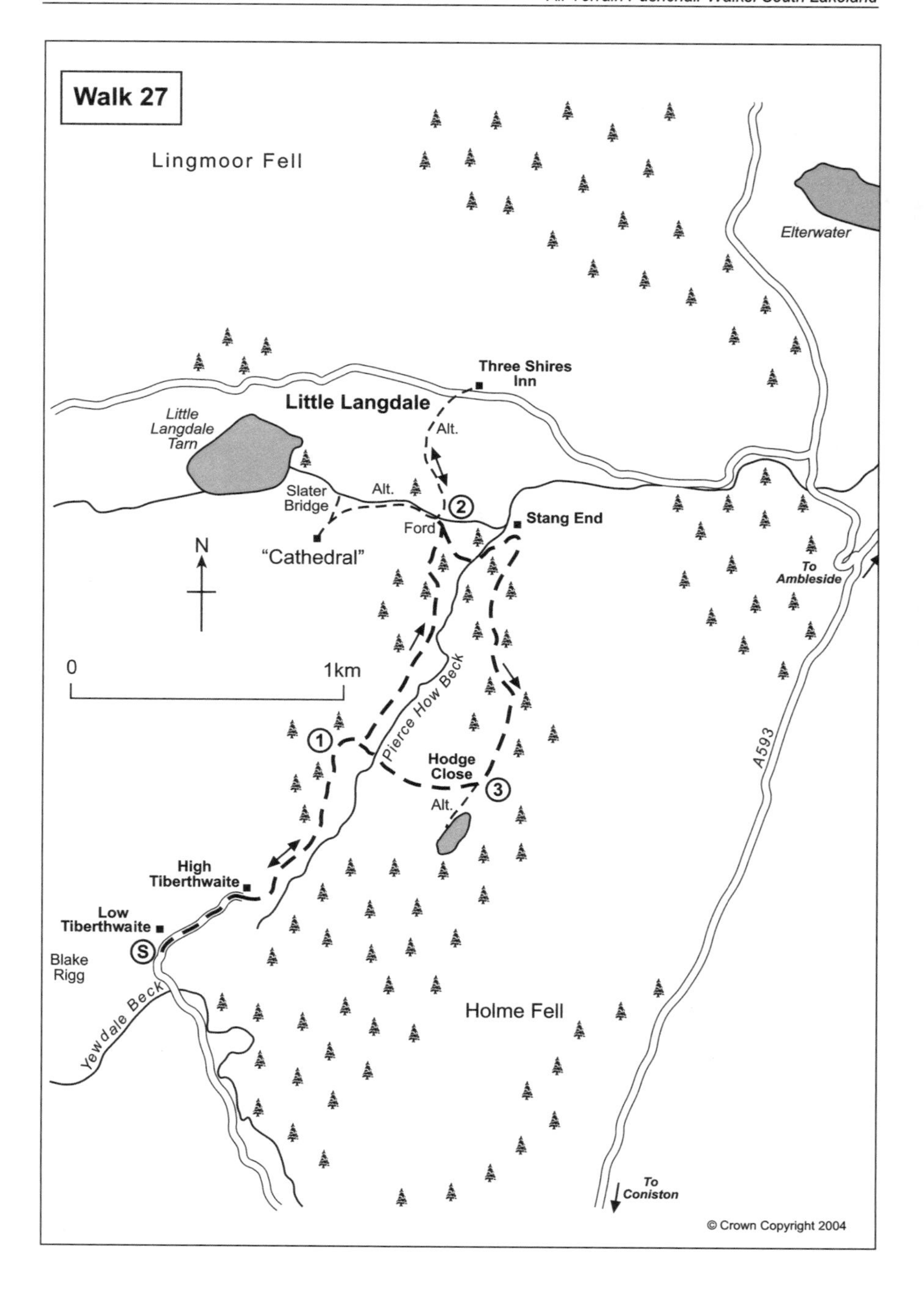

Walk 27
Lingmoor Fell
Elterwater
Three Shires Inn
Little Langdale
Little Langdale Tarn
Alt.
Slater Bridge
Alt.
2
Ford
Stang End
N
"Cathedral"
To Ambleside
0
1km
Pierce How Beck
1
Hodge Close
3
Alt.
A593
High Tiberthwaite
Low Tiberthwaite
S
Blake Rigg
Yewdale Beck
Holme Fell
To Coniston
© Crown Copyright 2004

junction of tracks. Bear left, following a 'Skelwith, Colwith' signpost, through the woods, crossing Pierce How Beck and passing a cattle grid before rising steeply to Stang End Farm. Pass between the buildings. Turn right at a junction, signposted to 'Hodge Close', rising quite steeply along a broad track. Go through a gate. Bear right at a junction and go through a gate into deciduous woodland. Pass 'Wythe Howe', go through a gate and keep right, along a tarmac roadway, into Hodge Close hamlet.

3. Towards the far end of the hamlet turn right to continue the circuit. (If you continue ahead for a comparatively short distance, you reach the enormous water-filled quarry excavation.) A broad, stony, track descends the valley side to a junction by a little stream. Go ahead, downhill, between stone walls, rough and wet for about 50m but soon improving. Cross Pierce How Beck before rejoining the outward route. Turn left to return to the car park in 1.2km (three-quarters of a mile).

Walk 28: Coniston Copper Mines

Assessment: Grade 3

The sole factor is the prolonged ascent. No problems with track surfaces or other difficulties.

Distance: 4km (2½ miles).

Total ascent: 135m (433ft).

Start/car parking: Pay-and-display car park in the village centre, with tourist information office and public conveniences, grid reference 303976.

Refreshments: Selection of inns and cafés in Coniston.

Map: Ordnance Survey Explorer 6, The English Lakes, South Western area, 1:25,000.

The Area

Generally as for Walk 29. This route goes to the heart of the Coppermines Valley former industrial area.

The Walk

Turn left out of the car park, passing the Donald Campbell monument. Pass the parish church, with Ruskin's grave, and join the main road through the village.

1. Cross the road, turning right and, in 30m, turn left, up the side of the Black Bull, home of the Coniston Brewery. Follow a surfaced lane, rising gently, with a stream to the left. The Yewdale Fells are close, to the right. The gradient steepens. Pass a 'youth hostel' sign as the road loses its tarmac

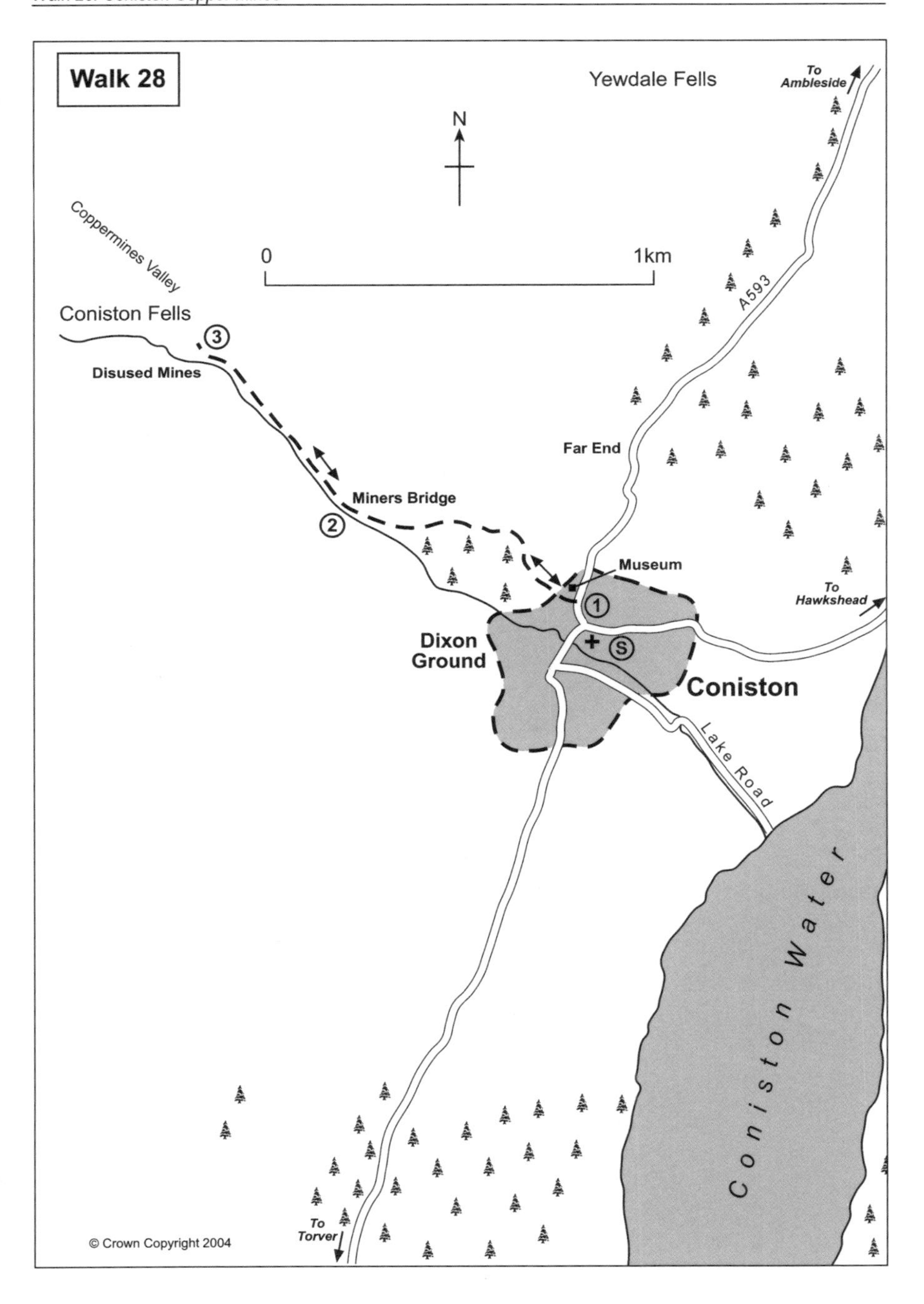
Walk 28
Yewdale Fells
To Ambleside
N
0
1km
Coppermines Valley
Coniston Fells
A593
Disused Mines
Far End
Miners Bridge
Museum
To Hawkshead
Dixon Ground
Coniston
Lake Road
Coniston Water
To Torver
© Crown Copyright 2004

surface and continue past a cattle grid, the stream now rushing along the bottom of a deep ravine.

2. Reach Miners Bridge, with rapids and falls, before the valley opens out into the historic industrial area of the copper mines. Carry on, soon reaching the youth hostel, holiday houses and an area with scattered mining relics. Attempts to create an organised mining museum on this site have so far had little success.

3. Return to Coniston village by the same route.

It is tempting to cross Miners Bridge and use the track descending on the far side of the stream as an alternative return route. This is *not recommended* for ATPs; the path is very rough in places and there is a tight kissing gate.

Walk 29: Coniston

Assessment: Grade 2

A generally easy, short walk on good surfaces, with only modest ascent.

Distance: 3.5km (2¼ miles)

Total ascent: 41m (135ft).

Start/car parking: Informal parking for three or four vehicles by the side of Lake Road, at the double bend close to the entrance to the workshops complex, grid reference 308975. Alternatively, use the main pay-and-display car park, with public conveniences, in the village centre or the parking area at the end of Lake Road, by the lake shore.

Refreshments: Choice of inns and cafés in Coniston.

Map: Ordnance Survey Explorer 6, The English Lakes, South Western area, or Explorer 7, South Eastern area, 1:25,000.

The Area

The large village of Coniston has a fine situation between the lake and the mountains, which include the popular Coniston Old Man. After the opening of copper mines, probably late in the 15th century, the area had intermittently thriving industry until the 20th century, served by a branch line of the Furness Railway from 1859 until closure after World War II. The industry has been replaced by tourism as the basis of the Coniston economy.

The origins of Coniston Old Hall are unclear; claimed by some to be based on a 13th-century defensive pele tower and by others to be of the 16th century. Although many of the building elements, such as the chimneys and the ramped granary are entirely typical of the area, as a whole it is unique. The present usage, partially as an office for the adjacent camping site, hardly does justice to the building. For many years Coniston Old Hall was the home of the Le Fleming family, also of Rydal Hall.

The Ruskin Museum, on the main street in the village, has been

Mountain scenery around Coniston Old Hall

extensively refurbished in recent years. Ruskin's grave is in the churchyard. Coniston's associations with the unfortunate late Donald Campbell are well documented, with a comprehensive exhibition of photographs and artefacts; there is a modest memorial close to the car park entrance and it is planned that Campbell's *Bluebird* jet boat will be restored and exhibited at the museum.

The Walk

Go through the double gate by the side of the roadway to the workshops, signposted 'Torver by the lakeside'.

1. Turn right immediately, along a good, firm, path, with a hedge on the right.

The views to the right are of the Coniston group of mountains, towering over the village.

Go through a gate and continue, crossing a stream and then through another gate, along a broad level track to a junction by farm buildings.

2. Carry on for a further 100m, through a gate, to Coniston Old Hall. Retrace the route for 100m back to the junction at point 2. Turn left, to follow the access drive gently uphill to a 'T' junction

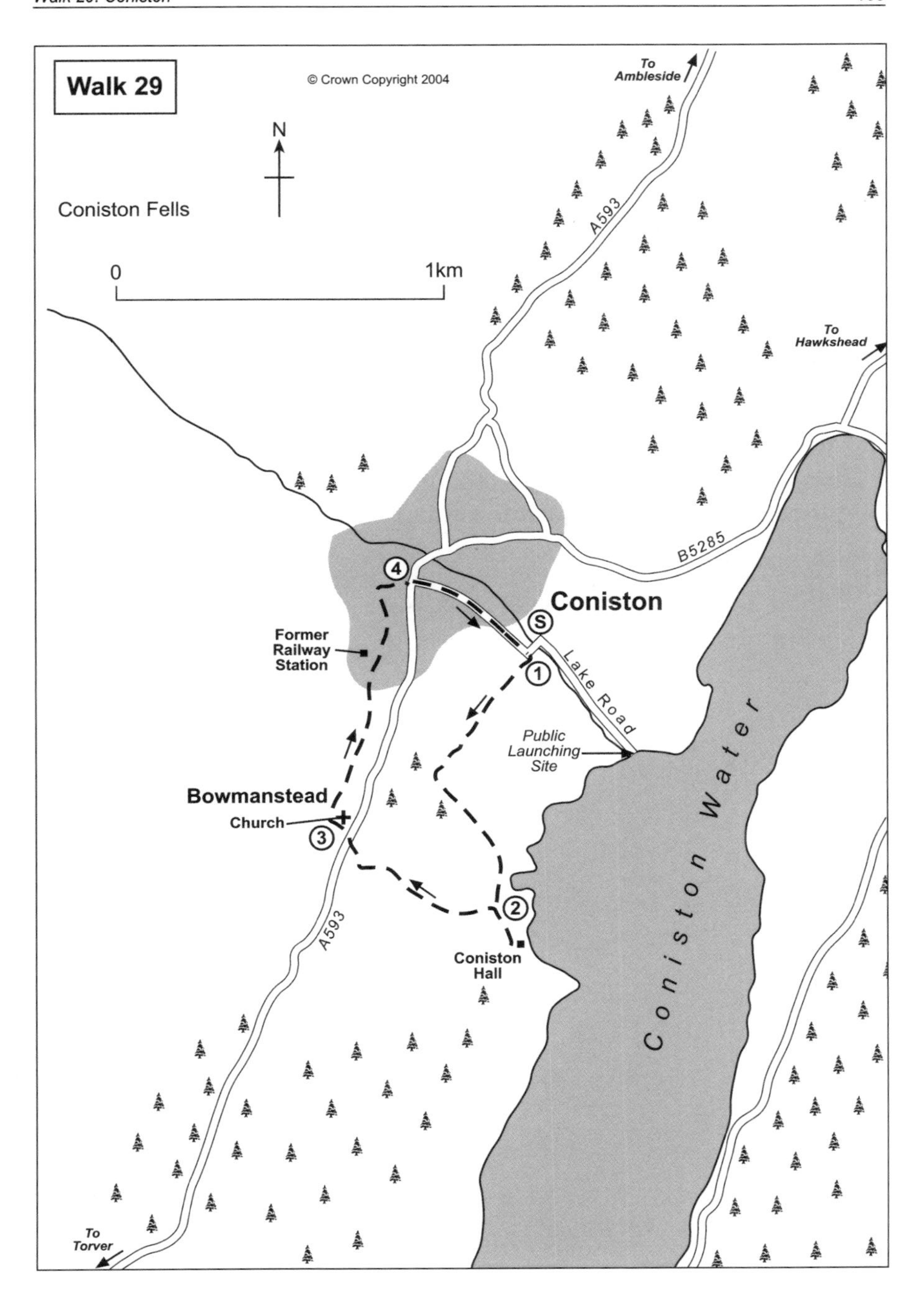
Walk 29
© Crown Copyright 2004
To Ambleside
N
Coniston Fells
A593
0
1km
To Hawkshead
B5285
Coniston
Former Railway Station
Lake Road
Public Launching Site
Coniston Water
Bowmanstead
Church
Coniston Hall
A593
To Torver

with a road. Turn right, soon reaching the main Coniston to Torver road. Cross the road then turn right towards the Church of the Sacred Heart, perched on a knoll.

3. Turn left, uphill, along a little road, passing under the former railway line. Turn right at a 'T' junction. In 30m, go through a gate on the right with a 'private land' sign. (The access is closed on the last Sunday of November each year). Turn left along the trackbed of the former railway line, pass a path giving access to the back of the Ship Inn, go through a gate and under a stone bridge, soon reaching a modern residential development. The area of the former railway station is to the left. Ignore a road on the left, continuing to a 'T' junction a few metres further. Turn right, downhill, along the roadside footpath; at a junction in 40m, continue down Station Road. The Sun Inn is to the left.

4. Go straight across the main road at the bottom, to follow 'Lake Road, leading to Beck Yeat', passing a small children's play area before reaching the parking area.

Walk 30: Windermere

Assessment: Grade 2

A fairly short walk, with a modest amount of ascent. Generally good underfoot, but with one section of narrow path by the lakeside and a narrow boardwalk, with a few steps, by the Sea Cadet hut.

Distance: 4km (2½ miles).

Total ascent: 60m (197ft).

Start/car parking: Roadside spaces at the village end of Birthwaite Road, immediately to the south of the village centre, grid reference 412983.

Refreshments: Cafés and inns in Windermere village.

Map: Ordnance Survey Explorer 7, The English Lakes, South Eastern area, 1:25,000.

The Area

This circuit links the village of Windermere with the nearest part of the lake, using semi-urban footpaths, some (quiet) roadside footpath and a delightful track along the lake shore. Of the combined Windermere/Bowness area, Windermere is the part less obviously attuned to the needs of visitors. A Victorian settlement, construction of the village centre followed closely on the opening of the branch railway line in 1847.

The Walk

Walk along Birthwaite Road, away from Windermere village.

> This is a relatively new road, constructed at a time when the local council wanted their own route to the lake, without having to pass through the territory of the rival Bowness council.

1. In about 400m, turn right, along a little path at a 'footpath' sign-post, soon reaching a wider lane. Turn left to continue through a

waymarked open gate to Birthwaite hamlet, which pre-dates Victorian Windermere. There is an old public footpath sign. The path continues past substantial accommodation for elderly people before joining the main A591 road, with St Mary's church on the right.

2. Turn left, cross St Mary's Park entrance road, then turn left again to follow another good path, descending gently among large houses. The track becomes a vehicular lane, still descending. A short distance before reaching the public road, keep left (main track) at a fork.

3. Go straight across Rayrigg Road.

A possible extension here is to go through a gate and take a track that rises easily to the top of Queen Adelaide Hill, a fine viewpoint owned by the National Trust .

Otherwise, turn right for a few metres, then turn left, through a gate, to descend fairly steeply by the side of Wynlass Beck. Cross a little bridge to reach the lake shore at Low Millerground, site of one end of a historic ferry route across the lake. The very old

Low Millerground

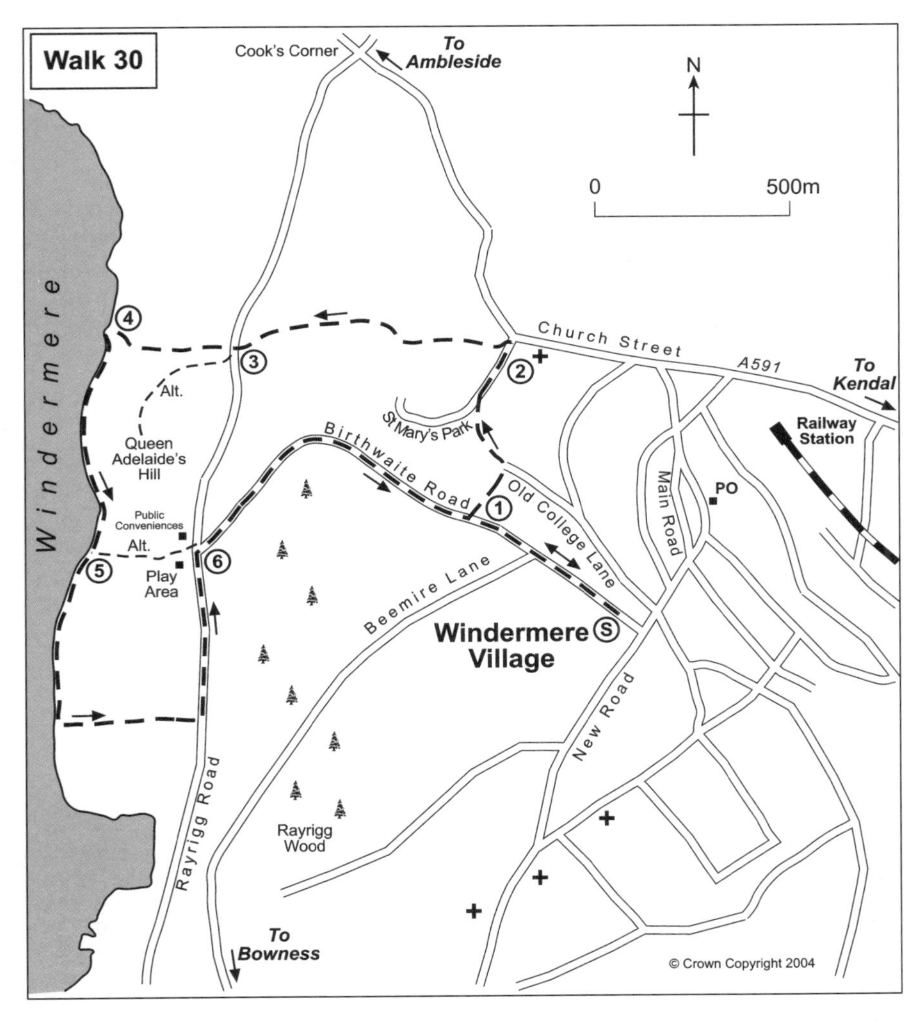

(17th-century) building on the left still has the housing for the bell which was used to summon the ferryman.

4. Turn left to pass behind a boathouse and carry on past the front of the Sea Cadet hut. The narrow boardwalk has steps at each end. The path now stays close to the lakeside, soon reaching Rayrigg Landings, with jetties and barbecue, a fine place for picnics.

5. **A left turn here shortens the circuit**, passing a children's play area and public conveniences on the way to Rayrigg Road. Cross the road to rejoin the full circuit at the bottom of Birthwaite Road, point 6.

   For the full circuit continue along the lakeside path, narrow in places, and with some tree root obstruction. Turn left through a gate, cross a broad meadow on a permissive path and join Rayrigg Road. Turn left to walk by the roadside for about 250m to the junction at the foot of Birthwaite Road.

6. Turn right to walk uphill by the side of Birthwaite Road, back to the parking place.

Also from Sigma Leisure:

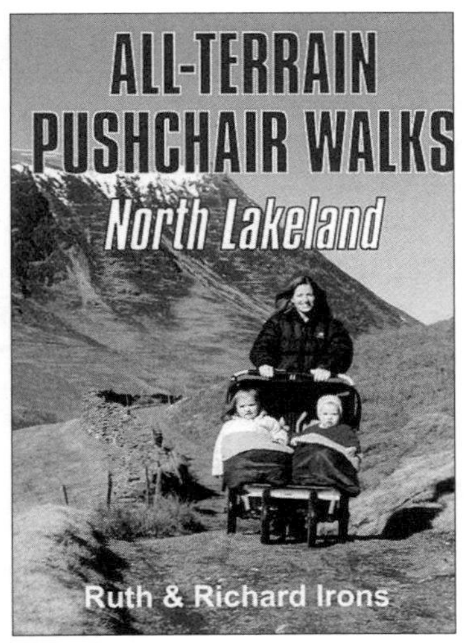

All-Terrain Pushchair Walks: North Lakeland

Ruth & Richard Irons

This was the first book to exploit the potential of the new breed of all-terrain pushchairs (ATP) – packed with sensible advice for first-time buyers and users of ATPs, plus information and tips for walkers with young children.
There are 30 walks across North Lakeland from Ennerdale Water to Lowther Park, Haweswater to Bassenthwaite. You'll find something to suit every type of walker – from Sunday Strollers to Peak Baggers and everyone else in between! Ruth and Richard Irons are experienced parents and qualified outdoor pursuits instructors – a reliable combination! *£7.95*

Other titles in our "All-Terrain Pushchair Walks" cover:

Anglesey & Lleyn Peninsula

Peak District

Snowdonia

West Yorkshire

Yorkshire Dales

Cheshire

All £7.95 each

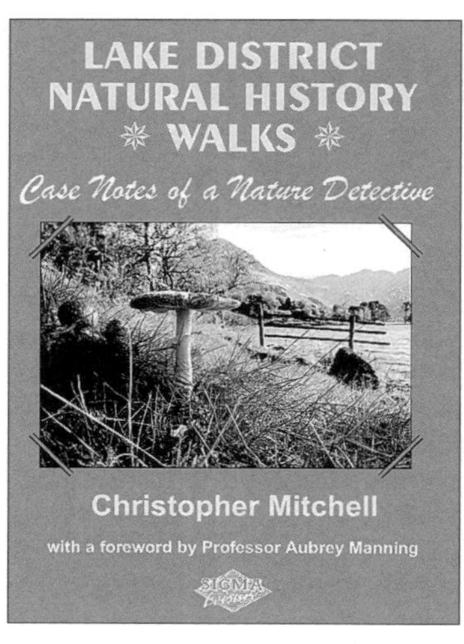

LAKE DISTRICT NATURAL HISTORY WALKS: case notes of a nature detective

Christopher Mitchell

Discover the Lake District's hidden wildlife, geology and archaeology. With 18 walks to choose from, readers can become nature detectives and solve the hidden mysteries. Detailed maps, clear drawings and photographs complement the text. *£8.95*

WALKS IN ANCIENT LAKELAND

Robert Harris

A collection of 24 circular walks ranging in length from 2 to 10 miles, each visiting sites and monuments from the Neolithic and Bronze ages, linked where possible with ancient trackways. All walks are accompanied by sketch maps, and the author's intricate hand-drawn sketches. *£6.95*

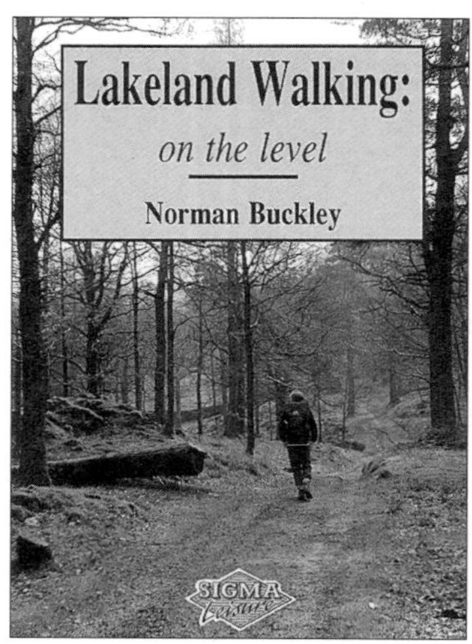

LAKELAND WALKING ON THE LEVEL

Norman Buckley

Walk among the highest mountains of Lakeland and avoid the steep ascents - with no compromises on the views!
"A good spread of walks" - RAMBLING TODAY. *£6.95*

EASY MILES, NO STEPS NO STILES – in & around the Lake District

Harriet Sharkey & John Barwise

Thee routes are ideal for pushchairs, wheelchairs and anyone who just wants an easy stroll. Easy Miles takes you to over 30 locations - some with spectacular views and others of special scientific or historical interest. Each route has clear numbered maps, helpful information and photographs to guide you along the walk. *£7.95*

All of our books are all available through booksellers. For a free catalogue, contact: **SIGMA LEISURE, 5 ALTON ROAD, WILMSLOW, CHESHIRE SK9 5DY**

Tel/Fax: 01625-531035

E-mail: info@sigmapress.co.uk Web site: www.sigmapress.co.uk